The ADHD Parenting Guide for Boys

From Toddlers to Teens—Discover How to Respond Appropriately to Different Behavioral Situations

Richard Bass

Table of Contents

Introduction

To be nobody but yourself in a world which is doing its best, night and day, to make you everybody else—means to fight the hardest battle which any human being can fight. –E.E. Cummings

Raising a child with ADHD is not easy, and many times friends and family, even doctors and nurses, don't realize the amount of stress parents are constantly under. Boys with ADHD need to be watched and reprimanded, on what feels like a minute-by-minute basis.

Can you count how many times a day you have to turn your head and see what else your child has picked up, thrown on the floor, opened, closed, or broken? Or the power struggles you enter whenever you try to enforce discipline?

What's worse is that many parenting books, unfortunately, don't consider the unique symptoms of ADHD when instructing parents on how to communicate, nurture, and discipline their hyperactive and impulsive boys. This means that for the most part, you are left to experiment with your own strategies and figure out the best ways to help your child self-regulate.

Added to this stress is the unhealthy dynamic created at home and at school when your little boy struggles to have positive interactions with family members, school teachers, and classmates. The combination of being impulsive and having underdeveloped social skills makes it harder for them to control strong emotions, read social cues, or empathize with others.

As a coping mechanism, your frustrated child might resort to disruptive behaviors like throwing tantrums, saying inappropriate things, or physically attacking others due to feeling unheard and invalidated. Unfortunately, these disruptive behaviors are what many people refer to when they label ADHD as a "behavioral issue" rather than a neurological disorder.

So, what do you do when your child exhibits these developmental challenges and parenting them starts to feel like a losing battle? Well, the answer is not to give up on them—or yourself as a parent—but to slowly undergo the process of changing your perception of ADHD and its effect on your child's development.

Dr. Stuart Shanker, the author of *Self-Reg*, believes that there is no such thing as a bad child, only a child who hasn't learned self-regulation skills. In his book he writes, "See a child differently, and you see a different child" (Shanker & Barker,

2017). This advice is true to parenting children with ADHD, but can also apply to other areas of life too.

What you believe about your life, job, health, or child determines your attitudes, decisions, and general approach toward them. If you choose to see a problematic child, then no matter how they behave (even when they display typical naughty behaviors), you will respond with less empathy.

However, if you seek to understand your child, and separate the "boy" from the "disorder," you can be encouraged to see a different child: A child who was born with a unique brain, and requires extra support and guidance to learn what comes naturally for other children.

Changing your perception about ADHD and its impact on your child won't change the world, or how others interact with your boy, but it can positively boost your own sense of well-being, calm your fears, and empower you to create a safe environment, where your child can thrive.

The truth is that parenting isn't easy, let alone when you are raising a child with a disability. You are already doing the best you can, and throughout the course of this book, you will be taught how to go that extra mile and positively respond to your child's needs. Although hyperactivity and impulsivity can be disruptive, they are also manageable, and can potentially reveal strengths that are unique to boys with ADHD, such as being goal-driven, hyper-focused, a creative thinker, and energetic!

Reading this book will help you grow a new pair of eyes so you can see your child differently. You will also walk away with practical, age-appropriate strategies to help your child manage stress, resist extreme emotional reactions, and positively adjust to social expectations in different contexts (i.e., at home and school).

Chapter 1:

Raising Your Bundle of Energy

Everybody is a genius. But if you judge a fish by its ability to climb a tree, it will live its whole life believing that it is stupid. –Albert Einstein

What Type of ADHD Does Your Son Have?

Your little boy has ADHD. But what exactly does that mean? First of all, it means that they are part of the 9.4% of children in the US who have been diagnosed with a chronic neurological condition that impacts their learning, emotions, and behaviors.

Second, since they are male, they are more likely to develop hyperactive-impulsive ADHD, which is typically characterized by hyperactive and impulsive behaviors.

In the sister book, *The ADHD Parenting Guide for Girls*, we explored inattentive ADHD—the second type of ADHD that mostly affects females. However, what is important to note is that both boys and girls can sometimes exhibit both types of ADHD. For the purposes of this book, we will discuss the ways in which hyperactive-impulsive ADHD affects young boys aged 3–17.

When a doctor says that your child displays hyperactive and impulsive symptoms, what do they actually mean? Hyperactivity is the state of being constantly active, to the extent of not being able to sit still or focus. Some of the signs of hyperactivity may start to show up when your child is in preschool, but are clearly visible when they reach middle school. These signs may include:

- fidgeting when sitting on a chair

- getting up frequently to walk around or play

- climbing over objects like tables or sofas

- having trouble playing quietly, or doing quiet activities like reading or homework

- talking excessively, and often speaking over others

Hyperactive behaviors tend to be more disruptive in younger children due to their inability to self-regulate. They might struggle to sit still, listen to stories, or participate in group activities. The older children get, the better they become at managing hyperactivity. Teen boys, for example, may be able to sit still during class, but might show signs of restlessness.

Impulsivity, on the other hand, is the act of doing something without thinking about the consequences. In most cases, impulsivity is triggered by an urge or strong emotion that feels overwhelming and cannot be contained. Signs of impulsivity include:

- being impatient; difficulty sharing or taking turns

- interrupting others while they speak

- having strong emotional reactions when upset

- blurting out answers before hearing the complete question

- yelling, cursing, or saying inappropriate things

The combination of hyperactivity and impulsivity can lead to accidents or disruptive behaviors. For example, while climbing on top of the kitchen island, your child might fall and hurt themselves. Or when they are overstimulated in public, they might throw a tantrum.

Moreover, their inability to self-regulate can interfere with their ability to learn and build strong relationships with others. These symptoms can, in some cases, be early signs of co-occurring conditions like Oppositional Defiant Disorder (ODD). Research shows that between 45–84% of children with ADHD will meet the diagnostic criteria for ODD (Connor & Doerfler, 2009).

However, not all defiant behaviors necessarily point to ODD. The main difference between the two conditions is this: The child with ADHD gets triggered by stimuli in their environment and gets upset, while the child with ODD may intentionally look for opportunities to misbehave and break rules.

Seeing Hyperactivity and Impulsivity Differently

When you think of hyperactivity and impulsivity, the following words might come to mind:

- chaos

- trouble

- intolerable

- dangerous

- impolite

- uncontrollable

While these are all acceptable ways of viewing these symptoms, there is also another way of looking at them which can help you understand your son better. However, before sharing the alternative outlook, it is important to state that every child acts up from time to time, whether they are diagnosed with ADHD or not.

Every parent goes through the "terrible twos" and the "threenager phase" when a toddler acts like a terrorist. You will find yourself saying "No" a hundred times a day, pulling all kinds of angry faces, and taking your child in and out of timeout—but still see no changes in their behavior.

These defiant behaviors are normal for that age because your child is still learning what acceptable and unacceptable behavior looks like. They aren't being "bad," they are just being a toddler.

Just as much as we can empathize with a toddler being a toddler, we can also empathize with a young boy displaying signs of ADHD. At the core of hyperactivity and impulsivity isn't chaos or dysfunction, but excessive energy. According to the Merriam-Webster Dictionary (2019), energy is the capacity of acting or being active. It is the inner compulsion that motivates a child to take action toward a desired goal.

Displaying a lot of energy is normal for children. The only difference with a child diagnosed with ADHD is that the release of energy doesn't seem to end. From the time your child wakes up to the time they go to bed, they are constantly on the move.

The excessive release of energy becomes "chaotic" when it starts to feel overwhelming for your child. This typically occurs when your child feels stressed or anxious. What many people don't realize is that boys with ADHD are prone to stress and anxiety due to the sheer amount of adrenaline that is pumping through their bodies on an ongoing basis. Even when their external environment is calm, the flooding of thoughts and emotions in their mind can trigger anxiety, and produce a rush of energy.

The best way to avoid chaos is to help your child release their abundant energy in a safe way. Failure to release this energy safely, and through positive behaviors, may lead to acts of aggression like throwing objects, yelling, or uncontrollable emotional outbursts.

What the child is trying to communicate through these disruptive behaviors is that they are feeling overwhelmed and desire a sense of control. Young boys, even teenagers, don't always understand what is happening inside their bodies when they need a release of energy. All they know is that they feel uncomfortable and must do something to alleviate the pressure.

Channeling Your Child's Energy Into Positive Activities

Your child's abundant energy can be seen as a problem or an opportunity, depending on how you look at it. When you notice that your little one is flying across the house, perhaps it is a great time to go outdoors.

The aim is to help them release some of this energy by engaging in positive activities. The opportunity here is that you get to teach them creative, motor development, problem-solving, coordination, and self-regulation skills while engaging in fun activities.

Below is a list of positive activities that can help your child burn energy:

1. Participate in physical activities

The NHI recommends that children aged five and above receive at least 60 minutes of moderate to intense physical activity every day. There are different types of physical activity that your child might enjoy, like playing running games (i.e., tag, red light green light, etc.), jumping on a trampoline, or playing sports. Some hyperactive boys enjoy fast-paced, contact sports, like football, basketball, or karate, while others prefer solo sports like tennis or swimming.

2. Volunteer

Another positive activity is volunteering. What's great about this activity is that your child can choose the type of social cause they want to support, and how they would like to help. For example, if your child is a nature-lover, you can walk around the neighborhood looking for litter to throw away. If they enjoy cooking, you can prepare soup packs at home, then drop them off together at a local shelter. Through volunteer work, your child will also get to develop social skills and improve their emotional intelligence.

3. Enroll your child in creative lessons

Research shows that children with ADHD are incredibly gifted divergent thinkers. They gravitate toward tasks like constructing new objects (DIY projects), brainstorming, creating unique artwork, and using their imagination. Find local kid-friendly creative classes that you can enroll your child in, so they can release energy through mental stimulation.

4. Spend more time outdoors

Being in nature has a soothing effect on the mind and can boost overall moods. Hyperactive children who play outside have a safe outlet to release stress and anxiety, and regulate their nervous system. Set up fun outdoor activities for you and your child and ask them to help you prepare. Examples of fun activities include having a picnic, camping, completing gardening chores, or walking your dog.

5. Give your child age-appropriate chores

Another positive way to release energy is to give your child age-appropriate chores. Not only is this a great way to teach your child the importance of collaboration and following instructions, it can also boost their self-esteem and create an element of fun. Hyperactive children may be more receptive to chores if they are presented as competitions, so create chore challenges and make sure you have rewards ready afterward!

Boys with ADHD need more exhilarating and creative activities to feel calm and balanced. Find ways of incorporating some of the activities mentioned above as part of your child's daily routine. Remember, 60 minutes is the minimum amount of physical activity recommended for children on a daily basis. Use that as your benchmark when structuring your child's routine.

Help Your Son Release Emotional Tension

Not every young boy with ADHD feels comfortable expressing their emotions. Some choose to internalize their strong feelings, rather than releasing them openly. This may be due to cultural expectations that force boys to "toughen up" and avoid visible displays of emotion.

Toddlers and preschoolers may have the added burden of not being able to verbalize what they are feeling, which can be extremely frustrating for them. To communicate how they are feeling, they might frequently cry or show physical aggression.

Some boys, especially teenagers, may take it to the extreme and completely detach from their emotions. For onlookers, this can make them seem insensitive or self-absorbed. However, if you look at it from their perspective, it is simply an act of self-preservation.

Just imagine you were flooded with intense emotions but weren't allowed to show any signs of them. To reduce the intensity, wouldn't you disconnect from your feelings, until you found a better way to manage them?

If you suspect that your child may be suppressing their emotions, it is important to intervene. Some of the physical signs to look out for are complaints about stomach pain, headaches, or lack of appetite. You may also notice that your child's self-esteem has dropped. For instance, they might struggle to make friends, prefer being alone, tend to avoid new challenges, or have a negative perception of themselves.

Remember, emotions carry energy too; therefore, it is vital for your son to learn different ways to express how they are feeling and release tension. Teaching your child to express their emotions is about equipping them with the right language and creating an emotional safe space that enables vulnerability.

Below are five strategies that are useful for boys of all ages:

1. Role-play

Come up with real-life scenarios of situations that would trigger strong emotions. Keep the scenarios simple and relevant to your child's age and lifestyle. For example, you could ask them to imagine not being allowed to play outside, being yelled at by a teacher, or struggling to complete homework.

Ask them questions like what thoughts would run through their mind, what sensations would flow through their body, and what emotions they would feel. Assist little boys to verbalize their emotions by having flashcards with different labels and photos of emotions.

2. Study facial expressions

Purchase a few magazines and picture books and go through each of them looking for different types of facial expressions. Stop at each face and ask your child what emotion they see. If they are not yet able to verbalize emotions, have a deck of flashcards with you. Depending on your child's maturity, you can take it a step further and ask them to imagine why the person feels that way, and what clues in the background give that away.

3. Creatively express emotions

Some children enjoy expressing themselves through art. If your child looks stressed or tense, you can take out a few art supplies, like a big sheet of paper, coloring pencils, and markers, and ask them to draw what they are feeling. This creative exercise can help your child process and release strong emotions, and walk away feeling relieved. Besides drawing, older boys might enjoy creating poetry, song lyrics, or a dance routine to express what they are feeling. Be open to different forms of artistic expression.

4. Journal

Journaling is a therapeutic technique that is more suitable for older children who are able to reflect on their thoughts and feelings. Buy your child a notebook and encourage them to journal about stressful events that occur in their life, like being rejected by friends, failing a test, arguing with school teachers, etc. Journaling is a positive way for your child to release frustration and make sense of their own life experiences.

5. Model positive behaviors

Teach your child how to manage strong emotions by modeling positive behaviors. Be mindful of how you deal with stress and anxiety, as well as what you say when you are upset. Realize that your child will mirror your behaviors. For instance, if you would like them to be more open about what they are feeling, be willing to share how you are feeling when something upsets you. It is also important for your child to see you practicing healthy coping strategies, such as taking time for yourself, practicing breathing exercises, listening to music, or reading a book.

In order for your son to feel comfortable with their own feelings, you must feel comfortable embracing yours. Spend some time exploring your own emotions and identifying situations that cause stress and anxiety. Look deeply into those situations and figure out what exactly triggers your strong emotions. Could there be underlying fears or traumas that are still active in the background of your life? Continue to explore your emotions until you are able to accept and embrace your feelings, rather than avoiding them.

Recharge Your Batteries to Cope Better

Raising young boys with an abundance of energy can be exhausting for parents! Taking regular breaks to rest and recharge should be something that is done often to prevent parent burnout. Yes, parent burnout is a thing! It can be described as the state of being physically, mentally, and emotionally exhausted from parenting responsibilities. Early signs include:

- chronic fatigue

- chronic stress

- changes in eating and sleeping habits

- lack of motivation

- isolation

- feelings of inadequacy

- emotional detachment

Parent burnout isn't a new phenomenon; however, doctors finally have a name for it. For centuries, it has been considered "normal" for mothers to take on the bigger share of childcare than fathers. But with more women entering the workforce and having to juggle parenting alongside other career, home, and financial responsibilities, they are vulnerable to stress and anxiety.

According to psychologist Martha Horta-Granados, parents with poor coping strategies, low resilience, and low frustration tolerance are more likely to experience parent burnout (Zapata, 2021). To prevent burnout, it is crucial for parents to recognize the early signs and symptoms, and practice positive coping strategies, such as:

1. **Learn the early warning signs**

There are usually early physical and emotional symptoms of stress that occur before you get triggered. For example, you might notice you feel irritable, nervous, or discouraged without a reasonable explanation. Or, out of the blue, your heart rate accelerates, you feel light-headed, or struggle to concentrate.

When talking to your child, you may be impatient or judgmental.

The moment you recognize these early warning signs of stress, it is important to stop what you are doing and take time to cool off.

2. Schedule daily breaks

When raising a boy with ADHD, daily breaks are essential. Just as much as your son needs an outlet to release energy, you need time alone to recharge. Schedule daily five-minute breaks into your routine to give yourself a moment to decompress. These breaks can be taken when your child is busy eating, napping, playing, at school, or working on their own homework.

3. Plan ahead for stressful times of the day

Every parent has a specific time of day where their stress levels seem to peak. For some, it may be in the mornings when they are getting their children ready for school, and for others it may be in the afternoons when they struggle to get their children to sit down and complete homework. Having a well-thought-out plan on how to manage that stressful period of the day can reduce anxiety and frustration.

For example, if your child engages in power struggles whenever homework time arrives, you can have them start with homework as soon as they get back from school (after eating lunch), then make playtime a reward. The boundary would be: If they can sit down for 20 minutes and complete their homework, then they can have an hour to play outside (or get to participate in a surprise activity you have planned).

4. Improve your sleeping habits

Research shows that parents and children who get enough sleep are more resilient when facing challenges (Gordon & Barnes, 2020). As a parent, when you are well rested you are able to think clearly and be more responsive to your child's needs. The daily recommended amount of sleep in the US is 7–9 hours. Decide on your ideal wake time and count backward to see what time you should go to bed.

Improving your sleeping habits isn't just about keeping a bedtime schedule, but also being mindful of how you unwind before bed. If possible, allocate 30–60 minutes before your bedtime to calming activities like drinking chamomile tea, reading a book, playing soft music, or sitting outside in the garden. Avoid caffeinated and alcoholic beverages or sugary snacks, as they can keep you up at night or disturb your sleep.

5. Practice deep breathing

Abdominal breathing, also known as deep breathing, is a relaxation technique that can instantly reduce feelings of stress and anxiety. The aim is to take deeper and slower breaths to allow more oxygen to the brain. A simple breathing exercise to practice is called box breathing. Imagine that each inhale and exhale drew an outline of a box. Start by inhaling slowly for three counts, pausing for another three counts, exhaling slowly for three counts, then holding your breath for the final three counts. Repeat this pattern until you feel calm.

6. Have a good laugh

You may be someone who holds stress in their face, and tends to clench your jaws, tighten your lips, or frown often. Smiling and laughing can help you relieve facial tension, reduce stress hormones, and positively impact your moods. Learn to find humor in the everyday struggles of life by laughing at yourself, laughing with your child, and finding ways to bring a bit of playfulness to everyday tasks. Connect to your own inner child and be spontaneous in how you interact and play with your family. You can crack a few jokes, pull some funny pranks, and make family bonding time something to look forward to!

7. Revive your social life

Parenting is a full-time job, but it doesn't have to take up most of your life. Think of parenting as one of many hats that you wear. Besides being a parent, you are also someone's child, sibling, colleague, spouse, and friend. With better time management, you can find ways to revive your social life and invest in these important relationships.

For instance, every week or bi-weekly, you can go on a date night with your spouse, coffee with a friend, or plan an activity that involves your extended family. Since you are raising a child with a disability, it may also be great to connect with other parents who share similar parenting experiences and can offer you guidance and emotional support. You will find a number of ADHD support groups and forums online that you can be a part of.

Chapter Takeaways

- Young boys are more likely to be diagnosed with hyperactive-impulsive ADHD, which, among other symptoms, makes it harder for them to sit still and regulate their emotions.

- When these symptoms are not managed, they can cause a lot of disruptions at home and at school. To curb disruptions, you can help your child find ways to release the abundance of energy they are keeping inside.

- Not only is it important to help them release physical tension, you can teach them how to release emotional tension too. Since many boys with ADHD find it difficult to verbalize their emotions, partly due to cultural expectations, look out for signs of emotional suppression and present simple and creative ways to release strong emotions.

- Raising a boy with ADHD can be exhausting and parents—especially mothers—are more vulnerable to parent burnout. To prevent parent burnout, it is important to prioritize your well-being and take regular time-outs throughout the day.

Chapter 2:

The Number-One Trigger That Sets Your Child Off

High stimulation is both exciting and confusing for people with ADHD, because they can get overwhelmed and overstimulated easily without realizing they are approaching that point. –Jenara Nerenberg

What Is Overstimulation?

Imagine walking in a mega shopping mall, with echoes of thousands of voices, during the busiest time of day, having very little air conditioning, and being far from the exit. One word that might describe your experience is panic, and interestingly enough, panic is a commonly felt state by boys with ADHD.

This is due to a phenomenon called *overstimulation* that occurs when the ADHD brain is overloaded with sensory input. Unlike typical brains, it is not equipped to process a lot of sensory information at once. For example, walking in a quiet park on an overcast day might be relaxing for your son. But as soon as you add the brightness of midday sun, sounds of screaming children, and unpleasant smells coming from the nearby garbage truck, then the experience becomes overwhelming.

When your child is overstimulated, their natural stress response is triggered. In a matter of minutes, their demeanor can go from relaxed to irritated and uncomfortable. What many parents may not realize is that during overstimulation, the child's defenses go up and their environment feels threatening.

Think of the terror that comes over an infant's face when they hear a sudden banging sound, and for those split seconds, believe that their life is in danger. This same fear and sensitivity is what a child with ADHD feels when they are overstimulated. How children react when they are overstimulated varies. Some boys might become visibly unsettled and defensive. Their impulsivity gets the best of them and they may yell, curse, or become physically aggressive. Other boys may isolate themselves or deliberately avoid situations that might be triggering, such as the playground, bright outdoor spaces like the beach, shopping malls, or going to the cinema.

It is also worth discovering what types of sensory input your child has a low threshold for because many times, you may find that there is a specific type of sensory trigger they cannot tolerate. For example, some boys with ADHD may not have an issue with loud noises, but are extremely sensitive to touch.

Wearing certain fabrics, walking barefoot, or being hugged or kissed are some of the things that can make them feel deeply uncomfortable. It is only when you observe your child that you can learn more about their triggers.

Help Your Child Identify Sensory Triggers

When sensory processing issues are not addressed, they can affect your child's sense of comfort and safety and interfere with their daily functioning. For example, being yelled at by a teacher can be so disturbing that it makes it difficult for them to concentrate at school.

It also isn't healthy for your child to be on "fight or flight" mode for an extended period of time. Not only can it compromise their immune system (making them susceptible to physical illnesses), it can also worsen their ADHD symptoms.

From an early age, you can help your child identify their sensory triggers. This can be as simple as keeping a notebook on hand, and recording common sensations that your child finds uncomfortable.

Later on, you can teach them how to avoid their triggers through self-advocacy. For instance, you might teach them how to politely decline a peanut butter sandwich at a friend's house because they don't like the smell or taste of peanuts, or how to set physical boundaries so that they don't receive unwanted hugs.

Below is a list of common sensory triggers and a few ways to manage them:

Touch-Tactile Sensitivity

When your child is sensitive to touch or textures, the "feel" of objects or personal contact with another person can make them uncomfortable. Common triggers include:

- texture of certain foods and fabrics

- unwanted personal contact

- feeling of someone brushing their hair

- touching things that stick to their hands

Manage this trigger by going clothes shopping with your child and have them try on different types of fabrics. If they are sensitive to clothing tags, neatly cut them off with a pair of scissors. When it comes to textures of certain foods, prepare different meals at home and see which ingredients your child leaves on the plate or spits out.

Sound-Auditory Sensitivity

Sensitivities to sound can make your child react to different kinds of noises. It may not necessarily be a loud noise, although this is common. It is generally any sound that your child finds unpleasant. Common triggers include:

- high volume on the radio, TV, etc.

- hearing dogs barking

- fireworks

- hearing someone chewing or slurping

- being in a loud mall, party, or restaurant

You can manage this trigger by purchasing a pair of earplugs or noise-canceling headphones to block out sounds. Sometimes, especially when your child is out in public, you may need to understand their need to wear headphones. Perhaps you can set boundaries around when it is appropriate or inappropriate to wear headphones. (e.g., walking around the mall with headphones is appropriate, but inappropriate when they are in the company of friends or when a teacher is giving a lesson).

Sight-Visual Sensitivity

Your child may be sensitive to bright and vivid colors and light, or being in a cluttered environment. In general, they prefer being in spaces that are neat, organized, and don't have a lot going on. Common triggers include:

- bright lights

- video games

- cartoons and other TV shows

- cluttered environment (including a dirty place)

Some of the ways to manage triggers include encouraging your child to wear a hat or pair of sunglasses whenever they play outdoors, replacing fluorescent light bulbs with dimming lights around the house (or at least your child's bedroom), and monitoring your child's screen time (enforcing restrictions for certain overstimulating shows).

Smell-Olfactory Sensitivity

Different, unusual, or strong smells can be unpleasant for a child who is particularly sensitive to smells. This also means they can pick up on smells that are lingering in the air that others may not notice. Common triggers include:

- strong perfumes and colognes

- cigarette smoke

- fumes from a trash bin

- certain spices or food ingredients

You can manage these triggers by identifying what types of scents your child finds unpleasant. Pay attention to the fragrances that linger around the house, flower displays, and the spices you cook with. You can also judge based on how your child reacts. For instance, if they pinch their nose or feel like throwing up, notice where they are and what they are holding or standing nearby.

Taste Sensitivity

Lastly, your child may be sensitive to how certain foods or beverages taste. If this is the case, they will most likely refuse to eat those foods. Please note that this isn't a typical case of refusing to eat vegetables, but rather being disgust-sensitive to certain foods. Common triggers include:

- hot (temperature) food

- hot (spicy) food

- cold (temperature) food

- sweet, sour, or salty foods

- textured food (i.e., pureed, crunchy, or sticky food)

One of the ways that you can tell the difference between foods that your child dislikes and foods they are sensitive to, is watching their reactions. If they dislike a certain ingredient or food, they might push it around the plate, pick it out of a sandwich, or eat small amounts of it; although, when they are sensitive to it, they may cry or panic when they see it on their plate.

What Happens When Your Son Wants More (Not Less) Sensory Input?

Other boys with ADHD may have a different type of sensory processing issue. Instead of seeking less sensory input, they seek more. For instance, they may enjoy touching things or being affectionate with people. They may also have a high pain threshold and prefer playing rough with other children, without realizing they are hurting them.

Below are a few examples of sensory-seeking behaviors:

- enjoying messy types of play (i.e., hand painting, tumbling in the mud)

- chewing on clothing

- bumping into people

- licking or chewing on inedible objects

- rubbing body against walls

- spinning around in circles

- enjoying sunlight, strobe lights, and shiny objects

- enjoying being in crowded and loud places

- enjoying rough play like wrestling

Bear in mind that some children may exhibit both types of sensory processing issues, in different contexts. For example, they may have sound-auditory sensitivities, but enjoy and seek physical touch. This is why it is important to observe your child and learn what their triggers are, and what they crave more of.

Before exposing your child to more sensory activities, consider the safety and implications of engaging in those activities. Some activities like playing outside on the trampoline or obstacle courses are relatively harmless, while others may lead to dependency and social isolation.

For example, if your child enjoys visual stimulation, set boundaries around how long they can play video games, browse social media, or watch TV. If they enjoy physical touch, teach them how to respect other people's physical boundaries and when it is acceptable or unacceptable to hug, kiss, or stand close to other people.

You also don't need to feel bad for saying "no" to certain high-sensory activities like wrestling, which can be very dangerous for your child. There are always safer options that you can introduce your child to that don't carry the same risks.

For instance, if you have a zero-tolerance policy for rough play, you can enroll your son into a martial arts class, where they are trained to release energy in a controlled manner. Or if you don't want your child biting or chewing on inedible objects, introduce them to different crunchy and chewy foods and snacks during meal times, or ask them to help you prepare meals so they can sample ingredients during the process.

Please keep in mind that your child may become quickly bored of the same high-sensory activities, especially as they grow and reach teenage years. They may show interest in other sports, social events, foods, physical touch, and music. Do your own research and investigate how safe those activities are for your child. If they are still too young to engage in certain activities, look for alternatives. Nevertheless, experimentation is healthy and not something to shy away from.

Chapter Takeaways

- The number-one trigger that can set your child off is overstimulation. This occurs when your child's brain has trouble processing sensory input from the environment.

- Signs that your child may be overstimulated include crying, throwing tantrums, experiencing a panic attack, or isolating themselves. When this happens, your focus should be on identifying what stimuli triggered your child and removing it (if possible).

- Once you have identified your child's sensory triggers, it is much easier to plan ahead to prevent exposure. You can also teach your child self-advocacy when in public, such as politely declining certain foods that are triggers.

- It is also possible that your child might have a different type of sensory issue, where they crave more stimulation than less. Observe what type of stimulation your child craves and find healthy activities they can engage in. It is okay to set limits and prohibit certain high-sensory behaviors, especially when they are risky or inappropriate for your child's age.

The final chapter will include a list of sensory-seeking activities that you can introduce to your child.

Chapter 3:

How to Handle Your Child's Explosive Emotions Without Losing Control

The emotional impulsivity of ADHD can make it easier to fly off the handle, or blurt out hurtful things. –ADDitude Magazine

The ADHD Brain and Emotions

Emotional dysregulation is not included as part of the diagnostic criteria for ADHD. However, there is sufficient research to suggest that children with ADHD have a difficult time controlling their emotions.

A 2020 research study invited 67 young children between the ages of 10–14 to participate in a Mirror Tracing Persistence Task (MTPT), a computer game that measures distress and frustration tolerance. The children were divided into two groups: those who met the DSM-5 criteria for ADHD and those who did not have ADHD. Results showed that the group of children with ADHD were more likely to quit the task than the group without ADHD, which indicated lower frustration tolerance levels (Seymour et al., 2016).

One of the common myths about ADHD is that it is a behavioral disorder. The problem, as some people see it, is that children with ADHD simply don't know how to behave properly. A child who is seen having an emotional meltdown is sometimes mistaken for a child who is seeking attention. However, the real root of their emotional challenges starts in the brain.

ADHD affects brain functioning, which causes cognitive, emotional, and behavioral impairments. For example, due to impaired working memory, your child might overreact whenever they experience a strong emotion, since it feels just as intense as when they experienced the emotion for the first time. Moreover, impaired working memory can make it harder for your child to recognize and respond appropriately to the emotions of others.

Another common phenomenon that is unique to children with ADHD is known as *flooding*. This occurs when your child's brain is overwhelmed and completely overpowered by a temporary intense emotion. Just imagine that you were completing work on your computer and all of a sudden, your screen froze. You couldn't move your mouse, refresh your screen, or restart your device. For those few minutes (which could very well feel like a long time), you were helpless to the error that had occurred.

The same analogy can be used to explain the experience of flooding. For those few minutes (which feel like an eternity to your son), they are overpowered by a single intense emotion that leaves them feeling paralyzed. They cannot turn to coping strategies because that part of their brain that is responsible for logical reasoning is temporarily disabled. All that they are able to focus on is the single emotion that has hijacked their brain— nothing else seems to matter. This can explain why your child takes a long time to calm down and get back to their normal self after they have been triggered.

You may be wondering about the long-term effects of your child's struggle to recognize, process, and control their emotions. Below are a few to consider:

- **Battles with social anxiety.** Boys with ADHD, particularly teenagers, are at risk of experiencing social anxiety. This has to do with their fear of how others might respond to them after learning about their diagnosis or noticing differences in how they behave.

- **Avoiding unpleasant emotions.** Some boys may decide it is better to simply push down or deny their emotions instead of finding ways to cope with them. When this occurs, they may turn to avoidant behaviors like procrastinating for studying for tests, turning to music or some other distraction when they are feeling down, or mentally dissociating (disconnecting from their thoughts, memories, and surroundings).

- **Getting lost in emotions.** It is also possible for boys to do the opposite and focus too intensely on how they are feeling, to the point of reaching a state of panic. What often causes this is the inability to rationalize experiences, such as being able to recognize a real threat from an imagined threat.

- **Frequent mood swings or lingering sadness.** Living with a disability that affects how you think, behave, and relate to others can be frustrating and depressing. These feelings can be worsened by the fact that not many people (including those in the medical community) understand the nature and impact of ADHD, which makes getting help harder. These frustrations can be internalized and trigger a feeling of inadequacy and low self-esteem.

The good news is that emotional challenges brought on by ADHD can be treated. The process often begins with seeking a medical diagnosis, getting your child on the right medication (if applicable), and turning to various psychotherapeutic strategies to develop emotional regulation skills. The following sections will present age-appropriate interventions to help your child manage their explosive emotional reactions.

Age-Appropriate Strategies to Help Your Child Cope With Big Emotions

No child is born with self-regulation skills, and many times, these skills are not taught at home or at school. It is up to parents to step in and teach their children how to cope with stress and overwhelming emotions.

Of course, parents of children with ADHD may need to reinforce these skills a lot more than parents of non-ADHD children; however, what's good to know is that the strategies are the same. The best way to teach self-regulation skills is to be intentional. Use difficult behaviors as opportunities to present and practice the most appropriate self-regulation skill and provide emotional support. Doctors call this "scaffolding" the desirable behavior, and should be done continuously until your son can remember to practice the skill on their own.

For example, when you notice that your child is experiencing sensory overload at a social gathering, you can take them aside to a quiet room or area and ask how they are feeling. They might be old enough to describe their emotions or may need you to help them by offering suggestions (e.g., "Are you scared or angry?").

Thereafter, you can present appropriate self-regulation skills to calm them down, such as teaching them how to take deep breaths. First, show them how to complete a simple breathing exercise and ask them to follow you. Thereafter, challenge them to practice the breathing exercise on their own and praise their efforts. Repeat this process, over and over again, until it becomes second nature for your child to practice a breathing exercise when they are feeling overwhelmed.

With all that said, below are age-appropriate self-regulation skills that you can teach and reinforce to your growing child:

Boys Aged 3–8

Typical explosive behaviors you can expect from your toddler or preschooler are having difficulty sharing toys (snatching objects from others), throwing tantrums when they feel frustrated, lashing out at others, and playing rough. The best ways to help your child self-regulate during this stage of development is gently shifting their attention to a less triggering activity and teaching them various self-soothing strategies.

Below are five strategies that teach your child how to cope with overwhelming emotions:

1. Take a movement break

If your child is visibly upset, distract them by taking a movement break. If you are indoors, encourage them to join you outside for a game of tag, playing with the dog, or raking leaves. If you can't go outside, create exciting indoor challenges related to household chores, such as "Who can fold the most laundry?" or "Who can pick up the most toys from the floor and place them inside the toy bin?" Make sure the activities involve plenty of movement to help your child relieve tension.

2. Practice a breathing exercise

When your child is upset, they may hyperventilate, which causes them to get less air inside their body. Breathing exercise deliberately lengthens the breath to induce a state of calm; it encourages belly breathing, rather than shallow chest breathing. Since kids are not familiar with terms like "inhale" and "exhale" you can use different objects to teach them the process.

For example, purchase a bottle of bubbles and ask your child to take a deep breath then blow the bubbles for as long as they can. Another trick is to get them to lay down on the bed and place a stuffed animal on their belly. Ask them to move the animal up and down by taking deep and slow breaths. You can also assist your child by counting for them while they breathe in and out.

3. Practice noticing and naming feelings

Another great way to prevent flooding and distract your child from focusing intensely on their strong emotion is to get them to notice and name what they are feeling. Start by asking them questions about what they are feeling inside their body (e.g., "Is your tummy sore? Does your head hurt? Are your eyes making tears?") After they confirm, ask them how those physical sensations make them feel (e.g., "How does your sore tummy make you feel?" Lastly, validate their feelings by using their own words. You might say, "Yes, I can see that your sore tummy is making you feel sick. You don't look very well."

4. Take a time-in

Traditional time-outs are used to remove a child from the situation and hopefully get them to reflect on their behaviors. However, for children with ADHD, time-outs can feel isolating and confusing since they are not able to control their strong emotions or calm down on their own. Time-ins are a gentle way of modifying behavior. Instead of sending the child to an isolated corner or room to be alone, the parent steps aside with the child and consoles them until they have calmed down. Over time, time-ins can improve your child's emotional intelligence and reduce explosive reactions.

5. Find ways to cool down

If you notice an anxiety spiral beginning, act quickly and look for ways to cool your child's body temperature. Cold temperatures (below normal body temperature) can act as a "shock" to the body and counteract "fight or flight" mode. The cool sensation is also calming and can serve as a positive distraction from intense emotions. A few ways to help your child cool down is pouring them a glass of water, placing a cold and damp cloth on their forehead, asking them to suck on an ice cube, or encouraging them to take a quick dip in the pool.

Boys Aged 9–12

School-aged children and pre-teens are more aware of acceptable and unacceptable behaviors; however, that doesn't mean they will always cooperate with their parents. During this stage of their development, they are beginning to build a sense of self and formulate their own ideas and beliefs about the world. Some of the typical explosive behaviors they may display include frequent mood swings, refusing to follow the rules, deliberately provoking others, and refusing to take accountability for their actions.

At this stage, your child is old enough to learn executive functioning skills, which will help them later on in life. Executive function refers to mental processes that enable your child to plan ahead, focus on tasks, follow rules, reflect and modify their behaviors, and practice self-control.

Below are five executive functioning skills to teach and reinforce, so you can start seeing improvements in your child's behaviors:

1. Task initiation

Both you and your son might get frequently irritated by task expectations. On the one hand, you might be tired of having to remind them to get started on homework, complete their chores, or remember important deadlines. However, they might be annoyed with the constant nagging and micromanaging.

Teaching your child task initiation is about empowering them to be proactive in managing their time and tasks, so you can step back and allow them to work independently. The aim is to train your child how to complete tasks as thoroughly as possible, while avoiding distractions.

A great strategy to introduce is timing how quickly your child can complete given tasks. Write down their start and end times for each task and praise them for their effort. Set targets together for how many seconds or minutes tasks should take. For example, both of you might work toward:

- beginning a task within 15 seconds of receiving the instruction

- taking two minutes to gather all of the materials and resources required to complete a task

- taking 30 seconds to transition from one task to another

Positive reinforcement is a vital component in teaching task initiation. Praise your child for making good progress, even when they don't meet their targets.

2. Self-control

Getting angry or impatient is normal; however, when strong emotions like these are not controlled, they can lead to overreactions. Instead of being the one that always reminds your son to calm down or think before they act, you can teach them how to control their behaviors.

There are different ways to do this, such as teaching your child about cause and effect, which can help them understand that every behavior has a consequence. You could explore behaviors like yelling, and how they can lead to negative consequences. For example, yelling at another child at school comes with consequences, such as getting in trouble with school teachers or possibly losing a friend.

Go through a few hypothetical scenarios and ask your child what they think the consequences might be. Help them learn how to tell the difference between undesirable behaviors that bring the least and most consequences (i.e., getting them expelled from school).

Additionally, you can teach your child to read the room. Reading the room refers to adjusting your behaviors to suit the people and environment you are surrounded with. For example, when speaking to a parent, teacher, or doctor, you can remind them to practice good manners, like saying "please" and "thank you." Or when they are in a formal environment, like an office, church, or doctor's room, you can remind them to use their soft voice. Role-playing is a great way to practice how to behave in different social contexts.

3. Accepting and reflecting on feedback

It can be really tough for young boys with ADHD to accept feedback, no matter how "polite" it may sound. Due to bottling up many of their fears and frustrations, they are hypersensitive to any comment that might sound like an attack on who they are. However, as you know, feedback is a necessary part of self-growth—possibly the best tool for change.

The best way to teach your child to accept and reflect on feedback is to model non-defensive behavior. When speaking to them, validate their thoughts and feelings, even when you don't feel the same way. Say statements like "I hear you" and "I appreciate your opinion." When the roles are reversed (when you are expressing your thoughts and feelings) ask them, "Do you hear me?" and "Can you appreciate my opinion?"

You can also teach them that feedback is about identifying incorrect behavior and looking for solutions. It is never a direct attack on a person. For example, name-calling is not useful feedback because it doesn't speak to any behavior. Have them practice giving feedback on the meals you prepare or the outfit you have on. Deliberately make mistakes (i.e., adding too much salt in your food) and ask them to critique you. At the end of the exercise, praise them for giving valuable feedback that you can implement moving forward.

4. Tolerance of change

Another factor that might trigger explosive emotions is change (especially when your child doesn't see it coming). For example, your child might react negatively when there are unexpected changes to their routine, or new rules that are enforced without prior warning or discussions. They may also fear being expected to complete a task that is new and challenging, like studying for a big assessment or joining a social or sports club.

To avoid emotional outbursts or avoidant behaviors, have open and honest conversations about upcoming change and what your child can expect. It is never a good idea to plan surprises because you don't know how your child might react to them. Use various tools to prepare your child for what is to come, such as writing down a list of steps together, going through photos of the venue or event, showing them a picture of the new schoolteacher, or watching videos of an experience.

If your child has questions about the upcoming change, be willing to answer them. If the experience is new for you too, it is okay to say "I don't know." The truth is, we can never be completely prepared for change, and this is an important life lesson for your child to learn.

5. Self-monitoring

Self-monitoring is the process of questioning your behaviors and evaluating if you are making the right or wrong decisions. Due to their impulsivity, your child might speed through tasks without carefully completing all of the steps, or they might make a comment without recognizing the impact it has on the receiver.

The best time to teach this skill is immediately after your child has behaved improperly. Get their attention and ask, "Can you tell me what was wrong about what you just did?" If they are unable to recognize their fault, explain it to them using facts only. You might say, "I just saw you step inside the house with muddy shoes. Remember, muddy shoes need to be taken off outside." Thereafter, assist them in behaving the correct way by walking them through the desirable behavior, and offer positive reinforcement.

Boys Aged 13–17

Teenage boys are aware of what is expected of them. When they react explosively, it is usually because they feel powerless, invalidated, or disrespected. For instance, they may struggle to accept failure or rejection, or they may feel misunderstood by friends and family. Typical defiant behaviors they may exhibit include lying, cursing, engaging in power struggles, challenging authority, self-harming, and breaking rules at home and at school.

The best way to teach your child self-regulation skills at this age is to model positive behaviors. What they need more than being told what is right and wrong, is to see healthy behaviors modeled in front of them. Apart from being a good role model, it is also important to be mindful of how you communicate with your child, especially when disciplining them. Imagine that you are speaking to another adult, who demands respect and consideration.

Below are five strategies to help your teenage son self-regulate:

1. Teach delayed gratification

Delayed gratification refers to taking actions today that will bring positive future results. The reward is not instant, which means the task or situation may seem "punishing" at the time. Typical scenarios where your child may need to practice delayed gratification include studying for tests, doing household chores, or saving money. None of these tasks is particularly fun, but all of them can prepare your child for adulthood.

When teaching delayed gratification, start out by showing your child how to differentiate between urgent tasks, important tasks, and non-urgent/important tasks. Urgent tasks are those that need to be attended to quickly, such as feeding animals. The gap between receiving instructions and taking action is a matter of seconds. Important tasks are those that must be attended to before the day is over. Your child's routine will indicate which important task to start with.

Non-urgent/important tasks should not be considered until all important tasks have been completed. In most cases, these tasks are postponed to the following day or the weekend, when your child has more free time.

Below is an example of how you and your child might sort through tasks:

Urgent tasks:

- packing a school bag before bedtime

- making the bed when you get up in the morning

- arriving at the bus stop at a certain time

Important tasks:

- completing homework for the day

- studying for an upcoming test

- helping out with dinner

Non-urgent/important tasks:

- visiting a friend

- catching up on a TV series

- baking cookies

Non-urgent/important tasks are what test delayed gratification. Yes, the task may not be important, but it may be fun, relaxing, creative, and exciting for your child. Encourage your child to be patient during the week (or while completing important tasks) and treat the non-urgent/important task like a reward for their hard work.

2. Teach the value of money

When your child becomes a teenager, they start having financial needs. They may ask you for money to buy a gadget, go out with friends, or shop online. Instead of shutting down their requests, you can take the opportunity to teach them the value of money.

For instance, set a weekly or monthly allowance and show them how to budget for items. Using the urgent, important, and non-urgent/important list can be useful when deciding what to spend on right now or save toward. When their allowance is depleted, encourage them to earn additional funds through carrying out certain chores and requests. For each completed chore or request, they earn $10.

If your child asks for a big-ticket item that costs more than their allowance, show them how to save up toward it. Buy your child a piggy bank and let them decide how much they are going to put away each week or month. Encourage them to deposit funds in their piggy bank before they start spending (a great way to reinforce delayed gratification). You can even motivate your child by helping them create savings goals and using visual tools like charts or calendars to keep track of their progress.

3. Let them fight their own battles

The following stage after adolescence is adulthood. Much of your focus as a parent will be preparing your child for adult responsibilities. A great way to start is to lead from behind. Like a shepherd tending to a flock of sheep, be available for guidance and support, but not actively fixing your child's problems. Whenever they behave improperly, allow natural consequences to kick in. For example, if they talk disrespectfully to a teacher, allow the school to carry out its disciplinary procedures.

Get into the habit of listening to more than solving your child's problems. Validate their feelings and show empathy for what they are going through, but always leave the decision-making to them. Ask them, "So, what are your options?" or "What are you going to do about it?" Whatever solution they come up with, give it your support. It may not be a realistic solution, but that is for them to find out.

Your job as a parent is to create an environment where creative problem-solving can take place—and the first idea may not always be the best one. If your child responds with an answer like "I don't know," reassure them that at the right moment, they will instinctively know what to do. Here, you are teaching your son to trust their own gut feeling.

4. Teach negotiation skills

One of the benefits of empowering your teenager is that you boost their confidence and increase their self-awareness. An empowered teenager is able to question their behaviors, consider the needs of others (or social rules and expectations they need to follow), and set healthy boundaries to protect their own needs. Negotiation skills teach your child how to create win-win situations and strike a good balance between their needs and another person's needs.

Some parents avoid teaching this skill because they think it will encourage defiant behaviors, like arguing and refusing to follow the rules. However, this is not the case. Negotiation skills don't minimize the importance of rules, nor do they allow debate about rules. The rules that are set at home and in other public spaces cannot be challenged. However, that doesn't mean that your child cannot express concerns or challenges they may be experiencing, and ask for you to accommodate their needs.

For example, if your child dislikes washing dishes and throws a tantrum each time they are forced to complete that task, you can sit down with them and enter a negotiation. Start out by stating the expectation (i.e., washing dishes every night), then ask them to express what concerns or challenges they are facing that make completing this task difficult. Perhaps they don't like the sensation of putting their hands in dirty water or having to wash dishes in the evening when they would rather rest.

Based on their concerns or challenges, the next question you would ask is, "How do you propose we resolve this issue?" Being excused from completing the task is not an option since rules are non-negotiable. However, you can sit back and listen to their creative solutions to make the task less undesirable. For example, they might ask you to buy kitchen gloves to prevent direct contact with the water, or they might request washing dishes in the morning, rather than late in the evening.

Some of their suggestions may not work for you. For example, you may not like the idea of them washing dishes in the morning. You are welcome to disagree; however, only if you have an alternative solution. Avoid shutting your son's ideas down without having anything better to put on the table. If you are going to disagree with washing dishes in the morning, for example, you can suggest moving dinner an hour earlier so that your child isn't staying up too late. Continue bouncing ideas back and forth and offering alternatives until you are able to agree on a workable plan that satisfies both of you.

5. Encourage communicating about needs

If your son is misbehaving, it is a sign of built-up emotional tension. The best way they know how to express their feelings or grab your attention is through acting up. Instead of paying too much focus on their undesirable behaviors, create room for them to verbalize how they are feeling. By validating and responding to their feelings, you can restore harmony in their mind and body.

Most teenagers won't openly share their feelings until they feel safe and respected. Your job is to not force your child to communicate their needs, but instead make your relationship with them feel safe. This means practicing listening without projecting your own emotions or trying to fix the situation. Give them the chance to organize their thoughts and express themselves using their own words and ideas.

Another useful tip is to ask questions more than offering advice. For instance, rather than saying, "You need to focus harder at school," you can ask, "What do you think can help you focus at school?" The aim is to create space for them to share their experiences and sort through their thoughts, without imposing your own views.

Lastly, let your child know that you don't need them to be a "good boy" and have everything under control. Nobody is perfect and they shouldn't feel the pressure to present a perfect image. Tell them that you are available to listen whenever they are having bad days and you won't judge them for not being in the best shape.

Chapter Takeaways

- Boys with ADHD have difficulty processing emotions, which can sometimes lead to a flooding of intense emotions and explosive outbursts.

- When your son is between the ages of 3–8, they are still grappling with the idea of having feelings and the best ways to manage them. Teach them how to describe what they are feeling, shift focus away from the intense emotion, and practice self-soothing techniques.

- When they grow older and reach the pre-teen stage, they are more aware of their emotions, but lack the executive functioning skills to reflect on their actions, correct behavior, and practice self-control. Your job will be to teach them these vital skills, which will come in handy later in life.

- Teenagehood is a time when your boy prepares for life as an adult. What you teach them about self-regulation at this stage will influence how they face and overcome challenges in adulthood. Since teenage boys are more independent, they may not be swayed by your words; however, the behaviors you model in front of them have a significant impact.

- Instead of "teaching" your teenage son how to self-regulate, you can offer feedback for what they are doing right or wrong, and allow them to creatively modify their behaviors and solve their problems. Show them that you have full confidence in their ability to make the right choices and be a responsible young man.

Chapter 4:

Self-Soothing Strategies to

Help Your Son Manage Stress

and Practice Self-Control

In the midst of movement and chaos, keep stillness inside of you. –
Deepak Chopra

What Is Self-Soothing?

Self-soothing is a relatively new term that is used to refer to stress management exercises that an individual practices to make themselves feel better. What helps one child feel calm won't necessarily work for another child. This is why children are encouraged to find coping strategies that work best for them.

Even though the term is fairly new, the practice of self-soothing isn't. From the time your child is a fetus in the womb, they learn various ways to self-soothe when they are feeling uncomfortable. For example, scans have shown that a fetus gets into the hand-to-face position, where they bring their hands to their face and around their mouth, when seeking to feel calm. Some fetuses have also been seen to suck their thumbs; however, this reflex develops better after birth (Little Steps, 2020).

Other common self-soothing practices seen in toddlers and preschoolers are foot tapping, rocking, humming, and nail-biting. Unfortunately, these habits are often seen as signs of bad manners and discouraged. Without other alternative strategies, children are left without any real way of calming themselves down.

Boys with ADHD, who are prone to feeling stressed and anxious, can benefit from self-soothing. Turning to positive coping behaviors can help them manage strong impulses and increase their tolerance for stress and frustration. Self-soothing practices can also teach your child how to manage their emotions without pushing them down. During moments of distress, for example, they are able to remain open and process what they are feeling, using positive coping strategies.

Your child has the opportunity to learn how to successfully overcome difficult situations without losing control, and in the long-term, this can boost their self-confidence. The following three self-soothing strategies teach your child positive ways to manage stress.

Watch that your child does not use these strategies in excess, to the extent of avoiding dealing with unpleasant situations. For example, if you notice they get into the habit of spending hours alone, even when they are not distressed, they may eventually isolate themselves from others. Self-soothing strategies are meant to be temporary tools to allow a child time to breathe and calm down before addressing difficult situations and negative emotions.

Create a Safe Place

A safe place is a secluded area in your home that your child can retreat to whenever they feel overwhelmed. It is presented to your child as an alternative for lashing out, hitting or throwing, or exposing themselves to excessive stimulation. Whenever you notice a change in their behavior, you can suggest cooling down in their safe place. Of course, in order for this area to be a place that your child desires to retreat to, it must live up to its name and provide both physical and emotional safety.

Creating a safe place is a joint collaboration. As the parent, you get to choose which room or area around the house that your child can use. Make sure that it is a room or area that doesn't get a lot of foot traffic, so that nobody disturbs your child when they are taking time out. When it comes to decorating their space, leave the majority of decision-making to them. Ideally, you want the space to represent their personality, interests, and idea of "safety." Of course, you can offer a few items to make the place cozy, such as adding pillows and blankets. You can also suggest adding soft cuddly toys, notebook and pen, music player, and positive photos like a picture of their favorite pet or a poster with affirmations.

Go slowly when introducing your child to the concept. The last thing you want is for them to think you are sending them away for a time-out. Discuss what a safe place is, what it is meant for, and scenarios where it would come to good use. Get your child excited about the opportunity to decorate their safe place according to their own interests. You can even start a countdown a week earlier to the "launch" of the safe place (the more excitement you build around this concept, the less resistant your child will be).

Teach Positive Self-Talk

How your child speaks to themselves can affect how they feel about themselves, and the stressful situation unfolding. If they rehearse limiting beliefs like "I can't do this," or "I am a failure," they are less likely to remain resilient during difficult times. Positive self-talk isn't about saying what you wish for, but instead saying positive but factual statements about yourself. During challenging times, you might remind yourself of personal strengths rather than your weaknesses.

Teaching your child positive self-talk starts with assessing their judgment of themselves and the world. You want to find out, through casual conversation, what your son thinks about certain people, topics, and experiences. For example, on the ride to school, you can ask them how they feel about their school, teachers, classmates, or academic performance.

With these questions, you are looking to see whether their assessments are realistic (balance of good and bad), exaggerated (extremely good or bad), or downplayed (showing indifference or detachment). Below is an example of how each perspective would sound like:

- Realistic: "I enjoy school because I get to see my friends, but I don't like math class."

- Exaggerated: "I hate school. I can't wait until I can leave!"

- Downplayed: "Hmm...I don't know. I guess it's fine."

Exaggerated perspectives are unhealthy because life isn't black or white. Plus, if your child gets into the habit of thinking negatively all the time, they may talk themselves out of pursuing goals and becoming a better version of themselves. Downplayed perspectives aren't healthy either. In most cases, they mask your child's true feelings, which makes it harder for them to address real concerns.

Once you have assessed your child's judgments of themselves and the world, you can introduce the idea of positive self-talk. They may have heard about it before, but maybe it wasn't presented as a self-soothing strategy. You can choose how you would like to describe positive self-talk depending on your child's age. For a younger boy you might explain it as talking to yourself in a loud voice, and to a teenager as giving yourself a pep talk. Encourage them to ask questions about when and how to practice self-talk. If possible, have a few responses prepared, such as:

Question: How often do you practice positive self-talk?

Answer: Whenever you are feeling down or notice their mood changing.

Question: What are the steps to practicing positive self-talk?

Answer: There are various ways to do it, like speaking to a mirror, reciting positive affirmations, or speaking to yourself like you would your favorite pet. Choose the methods that feel most natural for you.

Question: Why is it important to practice positive self-talk?

Answer: Positive self-talk reminds you of your strengths, achievements, and progress, so you can feel good about yourself.

You can then proceed to teach your child an important positive self-talk technique: reframing negative thoughts and creating positive phrases. Negative thoughts remind your child of what they can't do, instead of what they can do. Or they cause your child to feel bad about strengths or qualities they don't have, instead of those they do have. Here are a few keywords that can help your child identify negative thoughts:

Keyword	Statement
Can't	I can't focus.
Don't	I don't have a lot of friends like my other classmates.
Won't	I won't be successful in life.
Shouldn't	I shouldn't be so hyper.
Always	I always get left out.
Never	I never get to go out with my friends.

After identifying negative thoughts, it is easier to reframe them and create positive phrases. This is as simple as stating the above keywords in the positive (e.g., changing can't to can), or you can encourage your child to imagine they were responding to their best friend and offering positive reassurance. Here are a few examples:

Negative statement	Positive statement
I can't focus.	I am feeling tired and need a short break to stretch my legs.
I don't have a lot of friends like my other classmates.	I have a few friends who love and accept me for who I am.

Negative statement	Positive statement
I won't be successful in life.	My life path may look different from other people, but it will be awesome!
I shouldn't be so hyper.	I need to find a positive activity to release this abundant energy.
I always get left out.	I am invited to events that others think I might enjoy.
I never get to go out with my friends.	I go out with my friends whenever I can.

Practice Mindfulness

Mindfulness is an Eastern concept that dates back to thousands of centuries ago. It refers to the state of being present and paying attention to what is happening right now. Cultivating presence has the power to lower stress and anxiety because of how it ends the cycle of overthinking and dwelling on "what happened" or "what will happen."

Due to their hyperactive and impulsive nature, your child may find it difficult to sit still and pay attention to what is happening right now. When teaching them how to practice mindfulness, you can use fun and engaging games, otherwise they may find the experience of being present quite boring. Some of the improvements you will start to notice after regularly practicing mindfulness include sustained focus, improved emotional regulation, and more balanced moods.

Here are four fun mindful exercises to try with your child:

1. Mindful poses

To help your child cultivate presence, you can help them become more attuned with their body through different stretches. Take your yoga mats or beach towels with you outside and lay them on the grass. Guide your child through various stretches like reaching to the sky with their arms or bending over and touching their toes. Hold each stretch for five seconds then slowly get back to normal position. Take this opportunity to practice deep breathing exercises between poses.

2. Activating senses

Go on a relaxing walk with your child and challenge them to tune into different senses, one at a time. For example, you can start off by asking them to look for five things they can see with their eyes, then asking them to mention four things they can hear with their ears. Encourage them to take their time identifying objects. The objective is to slow things down by allowing them to focus on specific information. If you find that they are rushing through the answers, deliberately walk, talk, and respond slower.

3. Gratitude jar

Practicing gratitude is another way to cultivate presence. It can put your life in perspective and learn to appreciate what you have. Reinforce the importance of gratitude by helping your child create a gratitude jar. Bring out an old mason jar and various craft supplies. Spend the afternoon helping your child decorate their gratitude jar using different kinds of material. Finally, take out small sticky notes and pens/markers, and get them to write down what they are grateful for, then fold up each and place it inside the jar. Encourage your child to pull out their jar whenever they are overwhelmed and need a little pick-me-up.

4. Racing heartbeat

Regulating your heartbeat can help you calm down after a stressful event. While slowing down your breathing can help you achieve this, so can mindfully listening to each thump and following the rhythm of your heartbeat. Fortunately, this exercise is very basic and simple to teach children.

Start out by having your child run around the garden once or perform 10 jumping jacks. The aim is to increase their heartbeat so that they can monitor it as it slows down again. When they have completed the short cardio exercise, find a place to sit down together and instruct them to close their eyes and place one hand on their heart (chest area). Ask them questions about their heartbeat, like whether it is slow or fast, soft or intense, and what sound it makes. After a few minutes, ask them if their heartbeat has changed, and how so? Is it slower or faster, softer or more intense?

End the exercise by explaining that when a person gets angry, their heartbeat naturally speeds up and feels intense, or makes a loud sound. However, the more relaxed they feel, the slower and softer their heartbeat becomes. Therefore, a trick to feeling better when they are upset is to find a quiet place and listen to their heartbeat until it gets slower and softer.

Chapter Takeaways

- Teaching your child stress management and self-soothing strategies can improve the way they cope with triggers. Whenever they are overwhelmed, for example, they have a choice on how to behave: Either they yell and throw their toys or retreat to their safe place.

- No child responds the same to self-soothing strategies; therefore, experiment with a few and help your child find the most suitable based on their needs and preferences.

- Before suggesting a self-soothing strategy, have a discussion with your child first. Share more information about the particular exercise and how it might help them calm down when they are feeling upset. You may even need to demonstrate how the exercise is practiced, so they are comfortable doing it on their own.

- Self-soothing strategies are supposed to be positive and stress-free, so never force your child to turn to them when they are not in the mood. It is enough to present the option and allow them to choose whether they will proceed with it or not.

The final chapter will include various exercises to help your child improve self-control.

Chapter 5:

Managing Hyperactivity With Predictable Routines and Healthy Habits

Sow a thought, and you reap an act; sow an act, and you reap a habit; sow a habit, and you reap a character; sow a character, and you reap a destiny.
–Samuel Smiles

A Predictable Life Is a Peaceful Life

What is common amongst children with ADHD (both boys and girls) is the need for predictability. They crave a consistent weekly routine that has very little (if any) deviations. For instance, if they are accustomed to playing for 30 minutes after school, they expect that every day. If you replace that activity with something else, like quickly dashing to the grocery store or requesting them to complete homework, they will put up a fight.

Predictability to a sensitive and hyperactive child represents safety. It is a way to balance their enormous amounts of energy and help them stay grounded. When your son is struggling to regulate their emotions and behaviors, being in a predictable environment can help them reduce stress and clear their mind.

One way to create predictability is to set a routine. Following the same sequence of tasks, on a regular basis, can help your child stay organized and improve time management. A routine is also an effective tool to teach your child self-control. Whenever they are feeling overwhelmed, they can shift their focus to tasks within their control.

You may also notice less power struggles when your child has a predictable routine. In their minds, there are certain tasks that must be completed on a daily basis, like brushing their teeth, doing homework, and completing their assigned household chore. Plus, seeing the rest of the family following their separate routines (e.g., Mom preparing breakfast and Dad doing school drop-offs) can be enough of an incentive to keep them devoted to their own routine.

The older your child grows, the more important routines become. Teenage boys, for example, benefit from having routine because it can help them manage multiple responsibilities and develop healthy habits. With the right routine, your teenage son can create and manage a healthy lifestyle, with very little assistance from you.

Developing Routines

Creating a daily routine sounds simple enough. All you need is a calendar and you are good to go. But the problem many parents face is creating the right routine for their children—one that they actually enjoy and feel comfortable practicing on a consistent basis.

Your child is unique and has very specific needs and preferences that many "basic" routines won't accommodate. Instead of enforcing a rigid structure in their life, consider your child's likes and dislikes, which times of day they experience high energy, what they prefer to do after school, and the best times to carry out tasks that require concentration. I can guarantee that after you have made these considerations, the routine you come up with won't look generic.

Below are three steps that can help you establish a custom routine for your child:

Decide Why You Are Creating a Routine in the First Place

Before you start adding tasks to your child's routine, take a moment and think about what you hope to achieve. Why is it important for your child to get on a routine, or update their current routine? What are your intentions? What do you hope to do differently this time around? It is also worth reflecting on how you desire your child to feel when carrying out their routine. Are you looking to provide more peace and stability to their day? Or boost their confidence and challenge them to take risks?

Write down your purpose for creating a routine below:

_____

_____

_____

_____

_____

Decide on the Type of Routine

The next step is to decide on the type of routine you are going to establish. Here, you have a few options. For instance, you can decide on setting a daily routine that covers morning, afternoon, and evening routines, or you can double down on a routine that guides your child through a specific time of day.

If you are introducing the concept of a routine for the first time, start out with a routine that focuses on a specific time of day (i.e., morning routine). Once your child has learned this routine, you can introduce a bedtime routine, until eventually they have a daily routine established.

Map Out Your Routine

Now that you have chosen the ideal type of routine, it is time to brainstorm various tasks, habits, or rituals that you would like to include. Bear in mind that these tasks, habits, or rituals will be carried out on an ongoing basis, so make sure they are simple and practical. It is also worth considering what currently works or doesn't work for your child. For instance, what are the activities they enjoy or tend to complain about?

Remember that, even though you are building this routine, they are going to be the one driving it forward. If your child is old enough, invite them to help you brainstorm practices to include. Getting their "buy-in" early on will lower resistance when you finally implement the routine.

After mapping the routine, find different ways to visually represent it. For younger children, you might print out a poster with pictures showing different activities or create a video to demonstrate how each activity is completed. Older children may be comfortable reading from a color-coded calendar or having a to-do list they can tick off every day. Place the schedule in multiple areas around the home so that your child is reminded of their expectations on a daily basis.

Expect a few hiccups during the first few weeks after implementing the routine. Your child is still getting familiar with the new structure and they may not always get the timing right. Older children may even resist doing certain tasks. Make it clear that all tasks are compulsory; however, they are welcome to reorder the tasks or adjust allocated time frames to best suit their needs.

Daily routines can be adjusted several times, but doing so requires a collaborative effort and effective negotiation from both of you. Refusal to complete any daily task will result in consequences.

Managing Your Child's Fear of Change

The aversion to change makes trying out new routines difficult for children with ADHD. They may understand why the routine is beneficial, but can't help but feel ill-prepared for the ways in which their sense of "normal" will change.

Embracing change takes a lot of mental and physical energy. Your child has the enormous task of learning and memorizing new practices and carrying them out on a daily basis. If they previously had less expectations to live up to, the new routine can be overwhelming for them.

For example, a child may refuse to attend extra science lessons after school because this wasn't expected of them previously. Plus, having to focus more time and energy on a subject they may not enjoy (or be good at) is not a great incentive. Therefore, even though they understand the benefit of taking extra science lessons, they will put up a fight each time they are forced to attend one.

This might cause a lot of confusion and frustration for you as a parent. As much as you desire to support your child in every way possible, the positive changes you try to implement are always met with resistance. The solution here is not to give up on the new routine, but instead to help your child develop their resilience muscles. Show them through your own perseverance and enthusiasm that change is the best thing that could happen in their life because it leads to growth and greater confidence.

Below are a few tips to practice whenever you are preparing for change or helping your child get accustomed to new routines:

1. **Give your child a heads-up**

Children with ADHD do not like surprises very much because of their need for predictability. Any surprise changes to your child's routine can feel like an ambush. Take the time to discuss upcoming changes and how they might impact your child. Try to paint a picture of life after the changes have been implemented, and reassure them that implementing these changes is for their own good.

2. Be considerate of their concerns

It is normal for your child to have doubts about upcoming changes. Like anybody, your child doesn't like the idea of leaving their comfort zone and embracing the unknown. If they express concerns, take the time to listen and validate what they are saying. Don't try to talk them out of their concerns or minimize them. Agree that it will be difficult accepting the new changes and they may take a while to adjust.

3. Avoid making multiple changes

When introducing changes, focus on one thing at a time. For example, if you want to update your child's morning routine, change one task (like waking up 30 minutes earlier) and leave the rest the same. Once your child has gotten the hang of the new expectation, look for another task to change.

4. Give your child options (if possible)

Another great way to prevent resistance is to include your child in the planning stage. Tell them that you are in the process of updating their routine and need some help deciding on which tasks to include. Let them make small choices, like whether to play before or after doing homework, or which household chore they would like to be responsible for. Avoid giving them too many options (two to three options is sufficient), otherwise they may not be able to make a decision.

5. Remind them of how well they have coped with other changes

When motivating new changes, remind your child of some of the changes they have successfully conquered in the past. Describe a few memories that demonstrate courage, confidence, and resilience. Reassure them that the upcoming changes are going to be challenging, but they have the necessary skills to manage them.

Positively Changing Habits Using the Habit Loop

The idea of creating a routine is to gradually teach your child healthy habits that have the potential to manage ADHD symptoms and reinforce positive coping strategies. Any behavior that is practiced consistently has the ability to become a habit. This is both terrifying and exciting, depending on the kinds of behaviors your child practices regularly.

If you observe your child's current routine, you will notice that they already have habits formed. For instance, they may have a habit of eating the same cereal in the morning, making the same comments about school, crying every time you attend a doctor's visit, or napping when they get home from school. You can categorize their habits as being "good" or "bad," "productive" or "unproductive," but at the end of the day all of them are built on the same structure, known as a habit loop.

The concept of the habit loop was popularized by Charles Duhigg, in his book *The Power of Habit*. It consists of three stages that behavior goes through before it turns into a habit. These stages include:

- **Cue:** The environmental trigger that causes the brain to turn to a specific behavior.

- **Routine:** The actual behavior that is carried out, in the same manner, each time.

- **Reward:** The pleasurable feeling or validation that is received after performing the behavior (the reward is what reinforces certain behaviors).

So, how does the habit loop work? Let's take the habit of your child throwing a tantrum each time they accompany you to the grocery store. The cue is entering the grocery store. The routine is asking for candy and losing their temper when the answer is no. The reward is getting your attention and manipulating you to change your mind (ultimately causing them to get the candy they were asking for).

The habit loop doesn't only reinforce negative behaviors, it can also teach your child positive behaviors too. For example, you can use the habit loop to teach your child how to self-soothe when they are feeling stressed, like when they are around a group of people. The cue would be attending a social event like a birthday or being asked to mingle with other classmates. The positive routine would be taking deep breaths or rehearsing positive affirmations in their head (e.g., "I am welcome here" or "I am a friendly person"). The reward would be feeling better about themselves, and subsequently having positive interactions with others.

There will also come a time when you identify a destructive habit and need to break the habit loop. Using the same three stages, you can help your child unlearn that habit, or at least make it so undesirable that they don't enjoy practicing it anymore (i.e., they don't get the same rewards whenever they perform the routine). There are three steps you will need to undertake when breaking the habit loop, which are:

Isolate the Cue

The first step is arguably the hardest because identifying your child's cues requires observation. In the space of an hour, there can be so many triggers or stimuli that your child reacts to. Therefore, finding the exact cue can be a process of trial and error. Below are a few categories to help you isolate the cue:

- location

- people

- emotional state

- time

- action that took place before the trigger

Pay attention to where your child is when the destructive behavior takes place, who they are surrounded by, what emotional state they are in, the time of day, and the immediate action that occurred before they were triggered. If you find recurring patterns, like the same behavior happening when they are feeling a specific emotion, then that (the emotional state) may be the cue.

If your child is at school whenever the destructive behavior happens, write an email to their teacher and ask the following questions:

- Where are they when this behavior normally happens?

- What activity or action is taking place?

- What time of day is it?

- Are there certain students or adults who are present?

- Are there specific people who seem to provoke them?

- What emotional state are they in immediately before the action?

Identify the Routine

The next step is to identify the destructive routine. This will be pretty straightforward since the actions will be consistent every time your child performs the routine. However, the value of this exercise is to look behind the behavior and figure out what emotional needs your child is attempting to bring forward whenever they behave that way.

For example, when your child yells at other people, they may be feeling unheard or disrespected. The emotional need they are attempting to bring forward is the need for validation and acceptance. Another example is when your child constantly challenges your decisions and refuses to follow rules. They may feel like you are trying to control them and take away their freedoms. The emotional need they are attempting to bring forward is the need for autonomy and a sense of identity.

Taking the time to identify the routine and look at what emotional needs are being brought forward can help you complete the final step, which is to experiment with different rewards.

Experiment With Different Rewards

After isolating the cue and identifying the routine, the final step is to experiment with different rewards. What is important to remember is that your child is not "loyal" to any particular behavior—whether positive or negative. What they are loyal to are the pleasurable feelings they get when they perform certain behaviors. This means that if you can incentivize positive behaviors, your child can unlearn destructive behaviors—however, being good needs to be more advantageous than being bad.

Since you are more clued up about the emotional needs behind your child's destructive behavior, you can find positive ways to respond to those needs, without them needing to misbehave. For example, if your child needs validation, you can increase the amount of praise and recognition you give to positive behaviors. This will teach your child that behaving well comes with plenty of rewards.

In the same breath, you will need to ignore or withdraw attention from negative behaviors. Whenever your child throws a tantrum, for example, continue with the task you were working on and pretend like you don't notice. Don't show any emotion on your face (whether positive or negative) or react to their behavior in any way. The lack of attention will eventually make throwing tantrums an unprofitable behavior, and they will instead seek to gain your validation from behaving well.

Similar to enforcing a new routine, breaking a destructive habit will take a lot of time and practice. Be prepared for power struggles and plenty of testing from your child. If they are strong-willed, they will continue behaving poorly even when all incentives have been taken away (e.g., even when you issue consequences for their behavior). However, your job is to remain consistent in your actions and never show signs of being frustrated by their behavior (remember, even seeing frustration on your face can be enough of a reward to continue behaving badly).

Chapter Takeaways

- Boys with ADHD don't do well with surprises because of their need for predictability. Due to their sheer amount of energy, they perform better in environments that are controlled and organized.

- One of the ways to create a predictable environment for your child is to set routines. These are specific tasks that are carried out each day, in the same sequence.

- Be intentional when creating routines for your child and think about what you hope to achieve and how you would like them to feel on a daily basis. When mapping out their routine, consider their likes and dislikes to prevent power struggles later on.

- It is normal for your child to have fears about embracing a new routine. To help them through the transition, start discussing upcoming changes well in advance and giving them the space to express their concerns. You can also include them in the planning stage by asking for their input and allowing them to make smaller decisions like how to order tasks.

- The advantage of creating healthy routines is that your child gets to learn positive coping strategies that can help them manage ADHD symptoms. These will later become habits that make their life run a lot smoother and reinforce important life skills.

The final chapter will include exercises to teach your child how to develop healthy habits.

Chapter 6:

Prepare Your Child for the World—Develop Social Awareness and Responsibility

Getting or giving anything is about social skills. The world is about being comfortable where you are and making people comfortable, and that's what social skills are. –Penelope Trunk

What Are Social Skills?

Social skills are the everyday methods we use to communicate with others. They help us understand how to react, interpret, and empathize with what is being said to us. Developing social skills increases awareness of what is happening around us, and the most appropriate ways to respond.

All children need to be taught social skills; however, children with ADHD can have a difficult time remembering or intuitively knowing how to respond in social situations. They may need to be reminded regularly to say thank you, look other people in the eye while talking, or be selective in what they choose to share in public.

The reason for these social challenges is the well-documented impairments to the ADHD brain's executive functioning. Improving executive functions is possible, but researchers predict that children with ADHD will experience delays. Nonetheless, the earlier you start to reinforce executive functions like learning to pick up social cues, the better your child's social awareness.

Peer relationships are an important part of your child's development. Through these relationships, they are able to learn how to cooperate, negotiate, set boundaries, resolve conflict, and empathize with others. Watching TV shows or reading books where social skills are taught simply doesn't provide the practice your child needs. However, many children with ADHD don't get the chance to practice social skills because of not being approached or welcomed in social groups in the first place.

Due to having social challenges, they tend to keep away from others, or face social rejection as a result of being misconceived as "cold," "rude," or "uninterested." This creates a vicious cycle where social challenges continue to go unresolved because of your child's inability to be social. Without solid peer relationships, they may find substitutes to real-life connection, like being addicted to technology, or they may decide to avoid social interactions altogether and save themselves further rejection.

What is important to emphasize is that social skills can be learned. For example, a young boy who struggles to speak in front of the class or ask questions because of their inability to initiate conversation is fully capable of developing these skills. They may need regular practice at home; however, with time, parents will see improvements. There are also various ways to reinforce social skills in everyday situations, such as:

- Discussing social norms in everyday conversation, such as how to behave in class versus on the playground, or what to say when greeting a stranger and how to respond.

- Observing behaviors of movie or cartoon characters and asking your child what they did correctly or incorrectly, and how they could have responded differently.

- Role-playing common situations that your child may encounter, and taking turns switching roles (i.e., they get to play themselves, then switch to the other person's role).

- Encouraging your child to share about their social interactions at school, such as who they are playing with, how they get along with other children, and any social challenges they may be dealing with (i.e., getting in trouble due to their symptoms).

- Playing interactive games that encourage cooperation, collective problem-solving, and taking turns. These may include games like Jenga, Pictionary, Uno, and Scrabble.

The Eight Stages of Man

Erik Erikson was a German-American psychoanalyst and developmental psychologist, who came up with eight stages of development that begin in childhood and continue into adulthood (Mcleod, 2018). He developed these stages through many years of experience working with children and adolescents in psychotherapy.

Each stage presents a psychological "crisis" that the child needs to resolve before they can naturally advance to the next stage. According to Erikson, failure to successfully navigate each stage is what leads to psychosocial issues later in life. Below is a breakdown of the stages and how parents can support children through them.

Stage 1: Trust vs Mistrust

The first stage is learned when a child is a baby, around the first two years of their life. The sacred bond between mother and child is what builds trust and makes a child feel secure. When a child receives consistent and predictable nurturing, they will develop trust with their mother, which will later reflect in other important relationships they form.

If their need for consistent and predictable nurturing isn't met, they may perceive the bond with their mother as unreliable, and develop a sense of suspicion or hesitancy when approaching other relationships. What parents can work on during this stage is being intentional about how they handle their children, and the ways in which they reinforce unconditional love and security.

Successful outcome = The child develops a sense of hope.

Stage 2: Autonomy vs Shame

The second stage occurs when a child is between the ages of 18 months and three years. A secure child will develop a sense of autonomy after discovering the various things they can do with their mind and body. For instance, they may fold their arms as a sign of resistance, or say "No!" when they don't approve of something. An insecure child, on the other hand, may be reluctant to assert themselves, out of fear of being scolded by their parents. Overly controlled or criticized children will develop a sense of shame rather than autonomy, and may show signs of a lack of self-esteem and dependency on their mother.

Successful outcome = The child develops willpower.

Stage 3: Initiative vs Guilt

The third stage begins from the age of three, continuing until they enter formal school. This is the time when a child learns how to tap into their active imagination, various ways to play with others, and how to take turns leading and following. For young boys, it is usually when they experiment with their own strength and may engage in behaviors parents and teachers find aggressive.

Since they will be having a lot more social interactions, particularly with other preschoolers, the purpose is for them to learn how to play responsibly, be cooperative in groups, and make decisions that are considerate of others. These skills teach a child how to take initiative and feel comfortable expressing themselves. When their self-expression or decision-making is criticized, or punished (e.g., when they are yelled at for asking questions), they can develop a sense of guilt and personal inadequacy. Too much guilt can make the child afraid of openly sharing their thoughts and feelings with others.

Successful outcome = The child develops a sense of purpose.

Stage 4: Industry vs Inferiority

The fourth stage starts around school age, when a child is learning to read, write, practice sums, and complete chores on their own. Both parents and teachers play an important role during this stage, as they are the ones who are able to impart skills. The child may start to notice differences between themselves and their peers, such as not being able to grasp concepts as quickly as other kids, or not being the "cool" kid on the playground.

How they relate to their peer group is what can either build confidence or cause a lack of self-esteem. The child may feel the desire to demonstrate competencies in some area of their life to gain the approval of their peers and develop a sense of self-respect. Parents can nurture this desire by enrolling their child in sports, drama clubs, art classes, and other activities that might help them build self-worth and reinforce vital life skills. Failure to do so may cause the child to start doubting their abilities, or believe there is something inherently wrong with them.

Successful outcome = The child develops competence.

Stage 5: Identity vs Role Confusion

The fifth stage occurs from 13–20 years old. It is the stage where a teenager transitions into an adult. One of the central themes in their life will be discovering who they are, and what they believe. It is common for the child to have doubts about what they have been taught throughout their life, or the rules they are expected to follow. While this may be seen as an act of rebellion, they are simply trying to build their own belief system and make sense of behaviors they have been blindly following.

When parents validate their child's feelings and allow them to disagree with or negotiate rules, they are helping them individuate, which is to build a separate identity from their parents. This shouldn't be confused with permissiveness, which is indulging the child's desires and having low expectations for their behavior. Parents are still responsible for providing a structured environment and enforcing discipline; however, they allow their child to explore their identity, ask questions, and assert their own beliefs.

Failure to establish a sense of identity and assert their own beliefs will lead to role confusion. In other words, they may not understand what function to play in society, what their passions and interests are, or what meaningful contribution they can make in the lives of others. Role confusion can cause a lot of anxiety and make the child feel unprepared for adult life. The parents' role is to encourage the child to explore different interests, hobbies, and occupations in order to decide what kind of lifestyle works for them.

Successful outcome = The teenager develops fidelity.

Stage 6: Intimacy vs Isolation

The sixth stage occurs between the ages of 18 and 40 years old. The major "crisis" for the young adult as they encounter new experiences is to form genuine intimate relationships with other people. For the first time, they are more eager to form long-term relationships with people other than their family members, and the success of these relationships lead to safety, compassion, and commitment.

Not every young adult is able to develop true intimacy with others or maintain healthy long-term relationships during adulthood. The conflict they may experience in relationships is, to some degree, caused by the early attachment developed with their mother.

For instance, if the man or woman felt safe, nurtured, and validated by their mother as a baby, they are more likely to be open and trusting in intimate relationships. However, if the relationship with their mother felt unpredictable and lacked the affection that children need to feel safe and cared for, they may avoid intimacy and fear commitment as an adult—which often leads to loneliness and isolation.

Successful outcome = The adult is open to give and receive love.

Stage 7: Generativity vs Self-Absorption

The seventh stage occurs during middle life, where the adult man or woman feels an inner calling to make a mark on the world. They may develop interests in mentoring or making a positive contribution to the lives of others. Following this inner calling leads to a sense of accomplishment, while the failure to act upon it leads to feelings of stagnation and being disconnected from work, family, and the greater community.

Successful outcome = The adult deeply cares for others.

Stage 8: Integrity vs Despair

The eighth stage begins at 65 years old and continues for the rest of the adult's life. During this time, they may reflect on their childhood, adolescence, and experiences of adulthood and determine whether their life has been meaningful or not. If they were able to successfully navigate and resolve these psychosocial crises (stage 1 through to stage 7) they will develop integrity, while failure to navigate and resolve some or all of these crises will lead to despair.

Successful outcome = The adult develops wisdom.

These eight stages of development should not be taken as a prescription on how to raise your child, but rather as a description of how your child's psychological mind might develop over time. There are many other factors that might impact how your child grows up that are not mentioned in these eight stages; therefore, see these stages as just one way of explaining the process of how your child develops a personality and learns important social skills.

Teaching Your Child Social Responsibility

Social responsibility refers to understanding how our actions impact others. When we are mindful of the consequences of our actions, we have the opportunity to change.

Peer relationships are an important aspect of your son's development, and how they carry themselves in social settings determines the impact they make in others' lives. No parent wants their child to be alienated from a group due to not being aware of how their actions negatively affect others. Therefore, teaching your child how to be socially responsible can boost their self-confidence and protect them from public scrutiny.

Social responsibility begins with accountability. Your child was not born with a sense of accountability—children in general aren't. For the majority of their childhood, your child is dependent on you to take care of their needs. This is why they might respond negatively to rules or being assigned chores.

They have never had to be responsible for their actions in the past, so why now?

The danger that many parents make is to think that their children are too young to be held accountable. This is simply not true. Yes, of course, the tasks that children are assigned must be age-appropriate; however, setting expectations for their behavior, at any age, is how they learn to become responsible. When your child behaves badly, for example, it is expected for a consequence to follow. The consequence is a tool used to emphasize the expectation of behaving well.

Accountability at home translates to accountability at school or other social spaces. This is because behavior that is reinforced at home is reinforced in public. Your child may not behave well all of the time in social settings, but they are more capable of self-correcting. For example, if your child is taught at home that it is impolite to speak over people, and consequences are issued each time they commit that behavior, they will be more conscious of allowing others to speak in social settings.

The same can be said about teaching your child how to cooperate and take turns during play at home, or how to respect the personal space of others. Holding them accountable to these behaviors while they are in a safe and comfortable environment gives them enough practice for when those skills are expected socially. The earlier you start to teach accountability, the better. Unlike teenagers, younger boys are less likely to challenge the need to pick up responsibilities and be accountable for their actions.

A great strategy to use when reinforcing accountability is to make it clear to your child that they are behaving responsibly, and that you are proud of them for choosing those actions. For instance, after your child completes a task, you can say:

- "I am proud of you for following through with your responsibility."

- "I like the way you handled that responsibility."

- "You knew that it was your responsibility to do that, and I am proud that you did it."

- "I am rewarding you with 10 minutes extra screen time because you followed through with your responsibility."

You can also explain what their responsibilities are by being specific. For example, you might say:

- "When you don't understand a concept in class, it is your responsibility to raise your hand and ask a question."

- "Since you wanted us to get a dog, it is your responsibility to feed it."

- "We all have household chores, and your responsibility is helping me prepare dinner."

- "When playing with your friend, it is your responsibility to share toys."

Being deliberate in pointing out tasks that are your child's responsibility makes them conscious of their actions. Giving rewards after they have carried out responsibilities is also a great way to encourage reliable behaviors. During conversations, you can also remind your child of your responsibilities too.

For example, in the morning around the breakfast table, you can remind them of your responsibility to go to work, or when they are struggling at school, you can reassure them that it is your responsibility to offer support and help them manage learning challenges. Your child will eventually learn that every human being, whether young or old, is expected to manage their share of responsibilities.

Chapter Takeaways

- Social skills are the tools we use to build and maintain relationships with others. As your child grows up, they will need to develop these skills in order to have positive interactions with their peers.

- Due to impairments to their brain's executive functioning, your child may find it difficult to pick up on social cues, empathize, or judge the most appropriate behaviors in social settings. However, this doesn't mean they cannot improve social awareness.

- Erik Erikson's eight stages of development is a useful model to explain how your child's personality and social skills improve as they grow older.

- As a baby, their primary need is to trust that you will take care of them, and as they grow, they start to desire more autonomy, competence, and a sense of personal identity. Successfully going through these stages helps your child become well-adjusted and secure in themselves.

- It is important to teach your child how to be socially responsible, which means being aware of how their actions impact others. The best way to teach social responsibility is to hold them accountable for their actions from an early age. Accountability starts at home and spreads to other areas of your child's life.

- Society already imposes expectations on children; therefore, it is only fair for you to start teaching your child desirable behaviors. Make it clear to them that they are expected to uphold certain behaviors, complete certain tasks, and treat others in a certain way. Successfully doing so qualifies them for rewards, but failure to do so brings consequences.

Chapter 7:

Walking a Mile in Someone

Else's Shoes

Empathy is seeing with the eyes of another, listening with the ears of another, and feeling with the heart of another. –Alfred Adler

ADHD and Empathy

Empathy is the ability to put yourself in someone else's shoes, and for a brief moment connect to what they might be thinking or feeling. This skill is incredibly difficult for any individual to learn, and many times adults show signs of lacking empathy.

What makes empathy difficult to learn is that it requires a great deal of emotional intelligence (EQ). We can describe EQ as the ability to recognize and manage your emotions, as well as to recognize and respond appropriately to the emotions of others. Children must be taught how to stop and notice their emotions, and describe what they are and the impact they carry. Doing this helps them become more aware of the same emotions displayed by others, and the potential challenges they may be experiencing.

Children with ADHD are unfairly described as lacking empathy. People are quick to perceive their distractibility, blank stares, or inappropriate responses to social cues as signs of disinterest or rudeness. However, this is not the case. Children with ADHD deeply care for others, and sometimes even more than neurotypical children, due to their sensitive nature. They desire to express compassion and understanding, but don't always get it right.

For example, it may not come naturally for your child to comfort you with a hug when they notice you are upset. It's not because they aren't a hugger (although this might be the case if they are sensitive to touch), but more a case of not being aware that you need a hug. You may need to clearly say, "Can I have a hug?" in order for them to respond with affection, otherwise they won't be able to instinctively react that way.

Another example is when your child says something inappropriate that comes off blunt and rude. For example, instead of validating someone's feelings (e.g., "I can imagine what you are going through"), they might question their decision-making abilities (e.g., "How could you be so stupid?") Some children, especially teenage boys, who are uncomfortable with their own emotions may react with goofy behavior in highly emotional situations. To others, this can come across as insensitive; however, it is really not meant that way.

Difficulty showing empathy can put a strain on your child's relationships. For instance, at school, they may be misjudged and bullied because of not being able to respond appropriately in social situations. Since boys are stereotypically not allowed to express their emotions, practicing empathy may also be something they find awkward or shameful. By reinforcing this valuable skill at home, you can help your child become more aware and comfortable with their own emotions and those of others.

Age-by-Age Strategies to Develop Your Child's Empathy

Empathy works when you are connected to your own emotional experiences. This is incredibly difficult for children to understand or practice, since they are still attempting to make sense of their own feelings. It is common for a child to be unaware of the feelings of others, or miss opportunities to express sympathy. However, like any self-regulation skill, empathy can be developed.

Below are a few age-appropriate strategies that can help your child become more empathetic:

It can be hard for preschoolers to see past their own needs. The act of "sharing," for example, is seen as a loss rather than something that can strengthen peer relationships. Furthermore, in their efforts to assert themselves, they may be harsh or act unkindly. At this stage, your child may need to be reminded to treat others as they would like to be treated.

Here are a few strategies you can practice at home:

1. Read stories

By listening to stories, your child can visualize different behaviors and how they might impact others. A storybook character who is unkind, for example, might end up losing their friends. While going through a book, you can also stop and ask your child how certain characters may be feeling as a result of the behaviors shown toward them.

2. Create a "We Care" package

A "We Care" package is a box containing items like tissues, chocolate, stuffed animals, and a note card, to comfort someone when they are upset. Both you and your child can collaborate in putting together a "We Care" package for home (make sure you keep it stocked), and one for classmates, teachers, or anyone else your child might recognize as going through a difficult time and needing love and support.

3. Correct behavior as it occurs

If you catch your child being unkind or aggressive toward other children, take action immediately. Pull them aside and explain why that kind of behavior is unacceptable. Use phrases like,

"How do you think the other child feels?" or "How would you feel if they snatched your toys?" to give them some perspective.

Avoid using aggressive tone or language when correcting your child, as this can make them feel guilty for asserting themselves, which isn't wrong. What was wrong was their choice of reaction, and this can be modified when your child believes they can do better next time.

4. Play emotion charades

Emotion charades is a fun and interactive game to play when teaching your child language to describe how they or someone else is feeling. To play the game, one person stands up and mimes a specific emotion using gestures and without talking. The rest of the people playing take turns guessing what emotion is being depicted. Whoever guesses correctly gets to stand up in front and mime another emotion. This game is suitable to play with the whole family.

5. Observe others

Watching people is a great way to learn how to read different facial expressions, as well as other nonverbal cues. You can take your child out to the park and spend time observing people. Help your child focus on specific cues, such as a child's crossed arms or head lowered to the ground, and what they might be communicating. For instance, you might say, "Can you see that little girl who is stomping her feet? I think she might be angry at her mother for calling "home time." What do you think she is feeling?"

Boys Aged 9–12

The best thing about the preteen stage is that your child is starting to build a sense of self. Their personalities may be more evident than ever before, and they are able to assert their needs, even if it means challenging others. Nevertheless, this can also mean that they are less willing to compromise, may offend others with their strong opinions, and may respond inappropriately in social situations. At this age, your child may need to be taught how to be mindful of others' boundaries and be more sensitive when someone is visibly upset.

Here are a few strategies you can practice at home:

1. Set boundaries

It is important for your child to feel safe in the company of others, otherwise they may not be able to open up to them. Help them create a list of social scenarios that make them feel uncomfortable at home and at school. The list may include having a sibling barge into their room, being expected to give someone a hug, or being name-called by a classmate.

A simple phrase you can teach your child is: "I don't like it when [mention upsetting behavior]. Please don't do that." For example, "I don't like it when you take photos of me. Please don't do that."

2. Respect other people's boundaries

Teach your child that people have likes and dislikes too. For example, their older sibling may not like it when the younger one plays with their gadgets. Or a classmate may not like it when they sit too close to them. One of the ways they can learn to respect other people's boundaries is to ask for permission whenever they want a certain response or action from someone. You can teach them to say:

- "May I have a hug?"

- "Is it alright if I play with you?"

- "May I see your toy?"

- "May I enter your room?"

- "May I sit next to you?"

Asking for permission won't always lead to the response they are hoping for, and this is perfectly fine.

3. Visualize loving interactions

Visualization has the ability to positively change behaviors. The more times you visualize a specific emotion and various ways it can be felt and experienced, the more attuned you will be to it.

Guide your child through a visualization exercise. Ask them to think of someone they love who lives in another city or state, and send them positive thoughts. Once they have become familiar with this script, you can ask them to think about a time when they felt upset and send positive thoughts to that version of themselves, or classmates who may be going through a hard time and need positive thoughts.

4. Create empathy maps

Empathy maps are a great way to prepare your child for future emotional situations, and how to behave at those moments. Get a large piece of cardboard paper and a few markers. On the page, draw four big circles and inside each one write the words: feel, think, say, do.

Suggest a real-life situation and ask your child to write down what they might feel, think, say, or do in that scenario. For example, if one of their friends felt upset because of being bullied, what would they feel, think, say, or do? You are welcome to coach them along the steps and offer ideas.

Help them recognize that it is not always easy to know what to feel or think during new, intense, or awkward situations, and sometimes it is okay to express not knowing what to do. For example, if your child doesn't know how to respond to intense emotion like crying or anger, they might say, "I can see you are upset and I am sorry you feel this way. But right now, I don't know what to say to make you feel better." Rehearse the different responses with your child so that they feel confident responding appropriately.

5. Teach emotional validation

Emotional validation involves recognizing another person's feelings without making judgments. It is simply allowing them to express themselves and not feel bad for doing so. You can teach emotional validation by helping your child listen without interrupting others. Play a game together where each person has a turn holding the "mic" (could be a wooden spoon). Whoever is holding the mic has the opportunity to speak, while the other person must listen carefully so they can repeat what was said.

You can also teach your child to be tolerant of different views and beliefs. For instance, when they don't agree with what is being said, they don't need to react by shutting down the conversation or proving why they are right and the other person is wrong. Emphasize that everybody is unique and sees the world differently, and despite obvious differences, they can still allow others to speak and express themselves.

Boys 13–17

Teenage boys feel a lot of intense emotions due to surging hormones in their body; however, most of the time they don't know how to handle their strong emotions. It is common for them to develop masking behaviors, like being stoic, aloof, or disinterested, as a way to protect themselves from having "emotion overload." At this age, your child needs to know that it is okay for them to have and express big feelings. The more comfortable they become with their emotions, the easier it will be to respond to other people's emotions.

Here are a few strategies you can practice at home:

1. Discuss current affairs

Get into the habit of bringing up current affairs with your child. Ask them questions about their views on the changes taking place in society. Explore the case study from multiple perspectives, including how the situation might affect businesses, households, and communities. You can also ask them to share potential solutions that can improve the situation.

2. Support social cause

Encourage your child to dedicate themselves to a social cause. Each year, they can select a different cause that matters to them. Find ways to get involved in local projects and raise awareness for the cause. Your child should take the lead with this initiative, although you can help them get connected with the right people who can help make a positive contribution.

3. Journaling

Journaling can help your child share their thoughts and feelings on paper. What's great about this practice is that it is private and can be completed at your child's pace. For example, each day or week, they can set a goal to complete a journal prompt about their day, challenges they are facing, or how they feel about upcoming events. No one else has access to these entries, unless they choose to share them. The purpose of the journal is to help them make sense of what they may struggle to express to others.

4. Sign up for acting classes

The grown-up version of pretend play is an acting class. If this is an activity your child enjoys, they may find it to be a great way to express themselves. What's great about acting is that your child gets to step into different roles and imagine what each character needs and desires. In real life, this can help them learn how to recognize the needs and desires of others.

5. Empty chair technique

The empty chair technique is an exercise therapists use to help clients see a situation from the other person's perspective. Two chairs are positioned facing each other, and the client takes turns moving from one chair to another, expressing how they feel from different points of view (theirs and the other person's).

Whenever your child is faced with an interpersonal conflict, such as being at odds with a friend or teacher, you can coach them through the empty chair technique. Ask them to sit on a chair and pretend that their friend or teacher was sitting on the other chair. Encourage them to express how they feel, from their point of view, for three minutes.

When the three minutes are over, tell them to take a deep breath and switch chairs. For the next three minutes, challenge them to respond as the other person, expressing how they might feel. Continue switching chairs until your child begins to have a fair and balanced view of the situation.

Practicing Empathy Through Assertive Communication

You want your child to be confident standing up for themselves, while being aware of how their words and behaviors affect those around them. Assertive communication is a great communication tool that can teach your child how to express their thoughts and feelings without resorting to aggressive or inappropriate language or behaviors. Over time, this can deepen self-trust and help them value their own boundaries.

The first step in teaching assertive communication is to define what it is, and how it differs from other styles of communication. A child-friendly definition of assertive communication is expressing your needs and concerns while being considerate of the needs and concerns of others. It is a balance between being clear about what is wrong or what needs to change, but gentle in how you deliver the message.

There are other styles of communication that children tend to use when relaying messages, which are passive and aggressive communication. Passive communication refers to avoiding expressing thoughts and feelings, out of fear of being judged or hurt by others. A child who is primarily passive will bottle their feelings and allow hurtful situations to go unaddressed. Once those feelings reach boiling point, they may have an unexpected emotional outburst, which may be disproportionate to the event that actually triggered it.

Passive communication can impact your child in the following ways:

- They may be afraid to stand up for themselves.

- They allow others to cross their boundaries.

- They have difficulty expressing their needs.

- They may speak softly or make unnecessary apologies.

- They avoid eye contact and walk with a slumped body posture.

Aggressive communication takes assertiveness to the extreme. The commonality is that both styles of communication are open and forthcoming when it comes to asserting needs. However, aggressive communication lacks empathy and consideration. An aggressive child, for example, may be quick to express their hurt feelings, but do so in a way that hurts the other person too. For example, their response to a child snatching one of their toys is to push them over, yell at them, or snatch the toy from them. These actions are usually done in the heat of the moment without much thought about the consequences of their actions.

Aggressive communication can impact your child in the following ways:

- They may have a tendency of dominating others (e.g., insisting on being in charge).

- They use humiliation, like name-calling or bullying, to control others.

- They tend to get upset very quickly and react impulsively.

- They tend to speak loudly and over people.

- They aren't able to listen and consider where the other person is coming from.

Assertive communication enables your child to address problems without compromising the quality of their relationships. They are able to show empathy for what the other person may be going through and seek to find a solution that can work best for both of them.

DESO Assertiveness Script

Conflicts are a natural part of relationships, and it is important to prepare your child for these inevitable events that may occur at home or at school. Stress the fact that being in conflict with other people isn't wrong, but how conflict is handled can sometimes be unacceptable. For example, conflict resolved by hitting others or calling names is unacceptable because it inflicts pain on others. The better approach is to resolve conflict through assertively communicating concerns, and discussing what can be done differently.

DESO stands for "describe, express, specify, outcome." It is a technique that can help your child share how they are impacted by others' undesirable behaviors and explain how they would like to be treated moving forward. By following this script, they are able to give the other person the benefit of the doubt (since everyone makes mistakes), but still hold them accountable to their future actions. For instance, the last step, "outcome," presents consequences if the other person's behavior doesn't change.

This technique may be more successful with teenage boys, due to their level of maturity and ability to identify their needs and reflect on their own experiences. Nevertheless, being able to open up to others in this manner can be uncomfortable and they may need a lot of practice in the mirror or with someone else to prepare for these types of conversations.

Below are the steps to practice the DESO script:

1. **Describe your concerns or what you don't appreciate**

The first step is to describe the situation, or in most cases, behavior, that made you upset. The key is to stick to the facts, since these cannot be argued. Mention what you saw or heard that was concerning.

A statement like, "You went into my room without asking for my permission" is a good example of how to describe your concern. It focuses on the actions rather than the individual and is communicated objectively.

2. Express how the behavior makes you feel

The second step is to express how that situation or behavior made you feel. What is important to remember is to own your emotional experience. Take some time to think about what emotions were triggered and the impact made. Use phrases like "I feel" to show the other person that you are aware and take full ownership of your emotions. For example, when expressing how you feel about someone entering your room without permission, you could say "I feel angry because my room is my safe place."

Another important consideration is to not assume the other person's intentions. For instance, don't assume they carried out their actions to intentionally harm you. Many times, people act without thinking about the consequences of their actions; therefore, it is good to give people the benefit of the doubt.

3. Specify the alternative behavior you would like to see

The third step is to specify the alternative behaviors you would like to see happen to correct the undesirable behavior. When suggesting alternative behavior, be considerate of the words you choose. Remember, this is not a demand, but a request. Saying "Don't come into my room again!" is a demand, not a request. The request would be, "Please may you check with me first before entering my room."

Ensure that the alternative behavior is realistic and easy to follow. Telling someone to write a 300-word motivation before they enter your room is not realistic or easy to follow. The instruction must be direct, but also considerate of the other person's time and energy.

4. (Outcome) Lay down the consequences if the behavior doesn't change

The final step is to lay down the consequences. This step is crucial in holding the other person accountable to new behavior. For instance, if they don't change how they act toward you, they need to know what will happen. You can use the "If…then…" technique to explain the consequences. For example, "If you enter my room without asking permission again, then I will stop playing video games with you."

The aim of presenting a consequence is not to scare the other person, but instead to show them that you are serious about protecting your boundaries. To avoid making empty threats, keep the consequences simple, realistic, and within your power to carry out. Parents may need to step in and regulate the types of consequences older siblings give to younger siblings to ensure that no bullying takes place.

Chapter Takeaways

- Symptoms like impulsivity and distractibility make it harder for boys with ADHD to understand and process their own feelings, let alone try to appreciate what others are feeling.

- However, missing opportunities to validate others or respond appropriately in discussions doesn't mean they don't care about how others feel. Boys with ADHD are extremely sensitive toward others, but they don't always know how to express their concern and show support.

- The good news is that you can start developing your child's empathetic bone when they are very young through various strategies that can help them recognize and describe their own emotions, as well as being sensitive to the emotional experiences of others.

- Furthermore, you can teach your child how to stand up for themselves at home or at the playground without resorting to aggressive behavior. This can be achieved through assertive communication. The benefit of this technique is that it seeks to strengthen relationships rather than tear them apart. A resolution is encouraged which allows both parties to walk away knowing how to treat each other better.

The final chapter will include exercises to help your child practice assertive communication skills.

Chapter 8:

The Positive Parenting

Approach to Manage Defiant

Behaviors

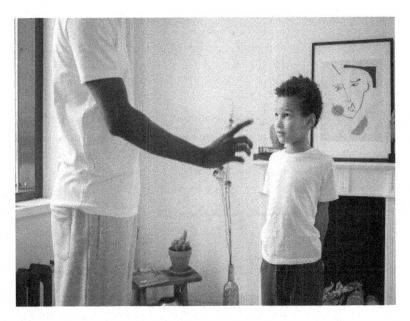

Stop trying to perfect your child, but keep trying to perfect your relationship with him. –Dr. Henker

The Reason Why Your Son Misbehaves

As mentioned earlier in the book, every child goes through several stages where they misbehave. If it isn't during the terrible twos, it is the threenager stage, or puberty. Boys with ADHD are more prone to mood swings and "acting out" than non-ADHD boys. It isn't that they act any differently from other children, but that they may be caught misbehaving more regularly.

Defiant behavior is not one of the symptoms of ADHD; however, as clinical psychologist David Anderson argues, it can be a result of negative patterns learned after years of being in conflict with adults. It is a known fact that children with ADHD get in trouble more often than non-ADHD children. Research has shown that by the time they are 10 years old, children with ADHD would have received 20,000 more negative messages than non-ADHD children (Jellinek, 2010).

Having this many negative interactions with others, specifically parents and teachers, can make boys with ADHD lash out and take extreme measures to protect themselves. You can think of these impulsive reactions as their defense against receiving more criticism. Boys who are more introverted may internalize their rage and develop avoidant behaviors like giving the silent treatment, avoiding interactions with people, procrastinating, or being passive-aggressive (i.e., being cooperative in front of someone but disapproving behind their back).

According to Dr. Anderson, "If you're being told from an early age that your behavior is wrong, or isn't what a kid is supposed to be doing, either you internalize it and you start thinking, 'There really is something wrong with me,' or you react aggressively toward the people who are telling you that you're wrong" (Miller, 2023).

Unfortunately for parents, boys with ADHD learn quickly that their avoidant behaviors work to get their parents' attention. When a child cries because they refuse to complete their homework, they know that the goalpost will be moved. Perhaps instead of expecting them to complete a whole assignment, their parent might ask them to do the first page, and they will finish the rest. Or when a teenage boy gets into a power struggle about what time they need to be back at home, they know that with a little more arguing, their parent will finally give in to their demands.

Therefore, it is important for parents to be empathetic toward their children's challenges, but in the same breath address defiant behaviors as they happen to show their children the acceptable ways for communicating their needs, expressing how they feel, and negotiating terms.

Traditional Punishment Won't Work

Not every form of discipline will work with your child, especially when you start to enforce discipline late (when your child has already developed their own ideas and beliefs about the world). Additionally, since children with ADHD are more prone to having negative interactions with adults, they may develop issues with authority, such as blocking out or minimizing whatever they are told by a parent or teacher.

One form of discipline that certainly won't work is traditional punishment, which refers to behavioral management strategies that have been used for centuries like smacking, isolating, or raising your voice at your child.

Since boys with ADHD are so used to being on the receiving end of criticism, yelling at them may not be enough to change their behaviors. In fact, the moment you start yelling is usually when they pull up their defenses and block out your voice.

Correcting behavior with aggression only instills fear, and as your child grows up, they may start to lose respect for you.

Traditional forms of punishment are also of no use in modifying behaviors of a child who constantly misbehaves. For example, if you are going to place your small boy with ADHD in time-out every time they misbehave, they may end up sitting in that corner for most of the day. The same goes for smacking your child whenever they are caught misbehaving. The only thing they register at that moment is the pain and violence, not the valuable lesson they need to learn to feel encouraged to behave well.

Another danger with traditional punishment is that it leads to short-term thinking. Whenever your child misbehaves, they become accustomed to receiving the same consequence, without understanding how their actions impact others, and how they can improve next time. All that it communicates is that your child was wrong, but doesn't explain why they were wrong and what the "right" behavior looks like.

To effectively correct your child's behavior, you may need to turn to modern forms of discipline that focus on teaching and reinforcing positive behaviors, rather than punishing negative behaviors. This form of discipline is gentle and considerate of your child's sensitivity to criticism, but still sets expectations (and holds them accountable) for how they should behave.

Five Types of Positive Discipline

Discipline is one of the duties of parenting that cannot be ignored. This is because what children learn about the world, and how to relate to others, is taught at home. Parents have countless opportunities every day to reinforce socially acceptable behaviors and steer their children away from socially unacceptable behaviors, so that when their children step out into the world, they have confidence in themselves to build relationships and navigate different social environments.

The experience of disciplining your child doesn't have to be negative or put a strain on your relationship. If you consider the definition of discipline, which according to Oxford Learner's Dictionaries (2023) is "a method of training your mind or body or of controlling your behavior," then you will see that it can actually be good for your child, and potentially strengthen your relationship.

To get the best outcomes from discipline, it may be necessary to evaluate your current approach. Are you still using outdated forms of discipline that are punitive and don't target bad behavior? Do you tend to be harsh or aggressive when correcting behavior? Or could your issue be the lack of consistent discipline, which causes your child to enter power struggles? Get clear on what you may be doing wrong that is making it difficult to modify your child's behavior. If you believe that you are doing everything right, but still unable to get through to your child, then it may be necessary to get them screened for ODD.

Considering you have found areas to improve, you can experiment with modern forms of discipline that seek to promote desirable behaviors, while minimizing focus on negative behaviors. Below are five types of positive discipline that are highly effective on children with disabilities:

Boundary-Based Discipline

Children need a structured environment to feel secure. Without this, they may not learn how to self-regulate. However, what is common with all children is that they will test the boundaries that you establish to see just how much they can get away with.

This isn't done to undermine your rules, but instead to discover for themselves where the limits lie and what acceptable and unacceptable behavior actually looks like. For example, you may set up a rule that nobody is allowed to yell inside the house. Your little boy may think to himself, "I wonder what would happen if I yelled inside the house." He may yell and watch to see what you are going to do about it.

Boundary-based discipline is about clearly communicating and holding your child accountable to the boundaries you have set. These boundaries are enforced whenever a child misbehaves, and failure to correct behavior leads to natural or predetermined consequences. For example, after hearing your child yelling inside the house, you would calmly walk up to them, get down on their level, and remind them of the rule.

You might say, "We don't yell inside the house. Please use your soft voice, otherwise there will be consequences." If they are strong-willed, they might yell again just to see whether those consequences are real or fake. With the same calm demeanor, you would walk up to them again, explain what they did wrong, and immediately enforce a consequence. For instance, you would say, "I told you that we don't yell inside the house, but you kept on yelling. I am now taking away 10 minutes of play time."

Gentle Discipline

Gentle discipline is about creating an environment that encourages good behaviors. This involves carrying out preventive measures to ensure that your child's needs and comforts are considered. A good example is creating routines to ensure your child gets enough sleep, active play, mind stimulation, and positive interactions with others. If you are aware of their sensory triggers, you would also make sure that these are monitored or kept away from your child.

To prevent power struggles, you could also adjust the way you communicate with your child. Instead of speaking harshly to them, slow down your pace, speak softer, and relax your facial muscles. You will still be able to set boundaries and enforce consequences; however, your message sounds more reassuring and is more likely to get a positive response.

Gentle discipline is also about showing empathy and anticipating your child's needs. If you notice that they are hyper and making a mess inside the house, that could signal the need to release energy. Without mentioning the mess they made, you would get their attention and invite them to a fun game outside. This strategy seeks to defuse stressful situations by addressing the underlying problem.

Positive Discipline

The ADHD brain seeks rewards and avoids any form of punishment. Focusing too much on what your child is doing wrong can feel punishing to them. They might get frustrated at not being able to live up to your standards. However, praising positive behaviors has a different effect. When they receive praise, it can feel deeply gratifying and do wonders for their self-esteem. Afterward, they are motivated to do whatever it takes to produce that same pleasurable feeling, which encourages them to self-correct bad behaviors and do their best to behave well.

Positive discipline is about using positive reinforcement to modify behavior. Examples of positive reinforcement include paying your child a genuine compliment, rewarding them for making good progress, and cheering them on when they feel down. When they misbehave, you can see it as an opportunity to get closer to your child, ask them how they are feeling, and what might have caused them to behave that way. Together, you can work on a solution to addressing the underlying problem, so that it doesn't happen again in future.

Emotion Coaching

Sometimes children misbehave because they are suppressing strong emotions, and looking for ways to express what they feel inside. For example, a child who throws a tantrum may simply be trying to get your attention because they feel neglected. Emotion coaching is about teaching your child how to recognize and express what they are feeling, so that you are able to respond to their needs.

Practicing this method requires that you first get to explore and understand your own emotions and triggers. You will find discussions about emotions a lot easier to explore with your child when you are comfortable opening up and embracing different emotions. Your child may also feel more comfortable being vulnerable around you when they see that you are more responsive.

You may also need to deepen empathy for your child. Instead of placing adult expectations on them, realize that they are still learning how to act right, show manners, or think with common sense. What is obvious to you certainly isn't obvious for them, and you may need to be patient while they train themselves to behave properly. Be quick to praise effort, even tiny modifications to how they behave, and slow to point out mistakes.

Behavior Modification

Similar to boundary-based discipline, behavior modification seeks to correct behavior by setting boundaries and enforcing consequences. However, the difference is in the emphasis that is placed on warnings and rewards. After setting a boundary, for example, you would issue several warnings (not more than three), each one sounding more serious than the last, to give your child an opportunity to correct their behavior. The aim is to teach them how to be responsible for stopping bad behavior on their own.

An example is telling your child to share their toys with their younger sibling, or else you will take the toy away. Make it clear to them that this is the first warning. If they don't self-correct, repeat the boundary with a more serious tone and tell them that if they don't change their behaviors, you will take the toy away. If they still don't stop, walk over without saying a word and carry out the consequence.

Rewards, on the other hand, are used to encourage good behaviors. Whenever you catch your child following a rule, working diligently on a task, or demonstrating good interpersonal skills, praise them with words, physical touch, or even tangible rewards. You can also use rewards when your child has successfully self-corrected their bad behavior. You might say, "Thank you for sharing your toys. I am really proud of you!"

Chapter Takeaways

- It is common for children to misbehave; however, those with ADHD tend to experience behavioral challenges more often. This has to do with their insistence on rewarding tasks and resistance to what they consider "punishing" tasks, like following rules, doing homework, being quiet in class, etc.

- Children with ADHD get criticized more frequently than non-ADHD children, which can make them more sensitive to criticism and prone to developing negative behavioral patterns, like yelling whenever they feel attacked.

- Responding to your child's misbehavior with aggression or outdated forms of punishment isn't the best way to correct their behavior. This is because they are so used to getting in trouble that adding more punishment won't teach them anything new.

- A better approach is to apply modern forms of discipline that seek to understand what your child is going through, how to respond to their underlying needs, and using positive reinforcement to motivate them to willingly improve their behaviors.

- To get the best results from these modern forms of discipline, start by evaluating what outdated parenting strategies you may be using that aren't being received well by your child. Just as much as there is room for your child to grow, you can also work on being a more empathetic, responsive, and encouraging parent.

Chapter 9:

Make a BIG Deal Out of

Rewards

Children who are accustomed to being treated well internalize that treatment and have a permanent sense of well-being. –Victoria Secunda

Your Child Craves More Motivation

A neurotypical child can train themselves to focus on tasks with little to no motivation. They may complain about the difficulty of the task, but manage to soldier on. This isn't the same for a child with ADHD.

Since the ADHD brain struggles to self-regulate, it requires a lot more stimulation to stay focused or complete a given task. For example, the best way for your child to learn information may be to use visual charts, watch videos, or anything else that can offer more stimulation than parrot learning or making endless notes. The same applies when your child is expected to complete a task. They would prefer if you disguised the task as a "fun challenge" instead of a routine chore.

The reason why the ADHD brain craves so much stimulation is due to the constant pursuit of dopamine, the "feel-good" hormone. Unlike typical brains, the ADHD brain cannot go long periods of time without excitement. Perhaps this is linked to hyperactivity, but one thing is certain—if it doesn't feel good, chances are high the ADHD brain won't show too much enthusiasm or dedication.

As a parent of a child with ADHD, it is important to realize that rewards are not a privilege for your child, but a necessity. Restricting the amount of stimulation offered to your child or positive reinforcement for good behavior will only produce a moody, argumentative, and unhappy child. Unlike non-ADHD children, they need rewards consistently, even during the process of completing work, as opposed to at the end. Short-term gratification is the one of the best incentives for their brain to stay alert and focused.

Nevertheless, the rush of dopamine can become addictive. The more stimulation your child receives, the more they crave. For older children, this can lead them to experiment in risky or self-destructive activities that provide an incredible "high" and ultimately cause dependencies. Rewards should therefore be contingent on performing positive and healthy behaviors, so that your child learns that living a healthy lifestyle feels pleasurable.

How to Set Up a Rewards System

If you are going to be handing out rewards on a consistent basis, it is worth creating a system that can help you monitor your child's behavior and take advantage of every opportunity to praise their good behavior. Having a reward system can also create more structure and predictability around when and how rewards are issued. In other words, they can be clear on what kinds of behaviors earn them rewards, on a consistent basis.

There are three steps that you can follow to set up a reward system at home:

1. Identify behaviors that matter

The first step is to write down a list of behaviors you would like to see more of. Perhaps there are a few behaviors your child struggles with, like self-soothing or cooperating with others. These are the kinds of behaviors that you should base rewards around, since that will encourage your child to be more aware of their actions.

Be clear and straightforward on the behaviors that qualify your child for a reward. For instance, "being quiet" is a vague expectation and doesn't give your child enough direction. The better expectation would be saying "using a soft voice when Mommy is on the phone."

2. Choose rewards that matter

Your child may be intrigued by the ability to earn rewards, but only if the rewards are worth it. Remember, your child's brain is on a constant search for dopamine-activating experiences. Thus, the rewards you offer must be exciting and special. For example, giving your child an extra 20 minutes of playtime won't really feel like a reward, since they don't have an appreciation of time like adults do. The more exciting reward would be to take a trip to the park or museum. There is a sense of adventure every kid feels when they leave the house and explore the city and this type of reward will certainly feel gratifying.

You can also consider the type of stimulating activities that get your child excited, such as:

- having a playdate

- watching TV

- not having to do their chores

- choosing which takeout to eat on the weekend

- visiting a theme park

- visiting their favorite ice cream shop

- earning extra pocket money

Avoid choosing rewards that are "too good to be true" or unmaintainable over time. For instance, promising a grand piano for getting an "A" on a math test is simply too good to be true. There is also the risk of your child thinking that each time they get an "A" on a math test, they will qualify for another grand piano! The aim is not to get your child's hopes up and fail to deliver on what you promised to do. Therefore, when deciding on rewards, think about how much time, money, and effort you are willing to invest on an ongoing basis without feeling any strain.

3. Enforce your reward system

Finally, your task will be to enforce the reward system. But before you do, discuss the upcoming changes with your child. Let them know that you are about to enforce a new system that rewards them for being good. Explain what behaviors you will be on the lookout for, and the types of rewards they can potentially earn.

Explain the step-by-step process of how rewards are given. For example, they may qualify for a single token (which can be exchanged for a tangible reward) after repeating the same desirable behavior three times a week. Use various tools to illustrate how the reward system works, such as pictures, diagrams, ladders, and pyramids.

Lastly, you can also decide on how to address undesirable behavior using your reward system. For instance, when your child breaks one of the house rules, you can consider deducting points as a consequence. If you are interested in this type of structure, make sure you explain what kinds of misbehavior lead to the deduction of points (once again, focus on those behaviors that you would like your child to stop urgently). Bear in mind that deducting points for negative behavior can feel punishing, depending on your child.

ADHD Behavior Charts

A behavior chart is a type of reward system that is suitable for preschoolers. It is a visual representation of desirable behaviors that qualify your child for rewards. The reason why this system is so effective for young children is due to how simple it is to follow. Studies have shown that these charts are effective at reducing disruptive behavior associated with ADHD (Aly, 2021).

Look online for inspiration when it comes to designing your chart. Print the chart on a large piece of paper (you can go a step further and laminate the chart to make it last longer). The chart should be visually stimulating (i.e., incorporating a lot of color and photography) and easy to read.

For instance, if your child is still learning to read, describe desirable behavior using short and simple sentences. Instead of writing "Carried out homework assignments" you can write "I finished my homework." Whenever your child performs a desired behavior, they earn a sticker. When they have accumulated a certain number of stickers, they get to choose a reward from the list.

Token Economy

Token economies work well for older children, who don't need pictures or simple charts to make sense of their reward system. It involves rewarding desirable behavior with tokens that serve as "currency" and can be traded in for tangible rewards. Tokens can be digital (i.e., writing down on a spreadsheet the number of tokens earned) or tangible (i.e., using stickers, marbles, or wooden chips).

The benefit of a token system is that it can monitor your child's behavior on a daily basis and provide them with continuous positive reinforcement. For example, they can earn a token for remembering to pack their school bag, making their bed, completing their homework as soon as they arrive home from school, etc. What this also means is that if they miss out on an opportunity to earn a token at any point, they have several more opportunities to redeem them.

In order to keep your child motivated, there must be a point where they can redeem their tokens for a tangible prize. It is best to sit down and negotiate with your child when this point will be, so that both of you are on the same page. For example, if your child is earning tokens at several points throughout the day, you may decide to reward them at the end of the day with a reward of the choice, such as:

- 15 minutes screen time in the evening

- dessert after dinner

- treat of their choice in their lunch box

- controlling the music playlist in the car on the way to school

- playing three rounds of a video game with a parent

If you decide on rewarding them at the end of the week, you can consider the following rewards:

- baking together

- playing their favorite board game

- going out to their favorite restaurant

- day off from doing chores

- getting to invite a friend over

Older children have more self-control than younger children, and they may decide to save up their tokens for a big reward that only comes after a month or several months. Both of you will need to decide what that big reward will be and how many tokens your child needs to earn to get it. Here are a few examples of big rewards:

- purchasing a new gadget like a cell phone

- purchasing new clothes

- earning additional money (this works well if your child has a big financial goal)

Furthermore, you can both decide on how many tokens each good behavior is worth. Ideally, the more desirable the behavior (e.g., behaviors that improve time management and organization), the more tokens your child stands to earn. The type of rewards they qualify for can also range depending on how many tokens your child has earned. For example, 0–50 tokens qualify them for "Tier 1" rewards, 51–100 tokens qualify them for "Tier 3" rewards, and so forth.

The token economy can also target bad behaviors through positive reinforcement. Instead of taking tokens away for behaving badly (although this is acceptable too), offer bonus tokens at the end of the day if the behavior was not practiced. To make this offer more attractive, make these bonus tokens the highest number of tokens that any behavior can earn (e.g., earning 10 tokens for not losing their temper).

Below is a basic template to help you keep track of the tokens your child earns on a daily basis:

Target behavior	Frequency of monitoring	Tokens earned
Waking up to the alarm at 06:30 a.m.	Check at 06:35 a.m.	2
Packing a school bag with all the necessary books and assignments	Check before my child enters the car	2

Target behavior	Frequency of monitoring	Tokens earned
Completing chores in the afternoon	Check if chores have been completed before I go to bed	4
Bonus: Does not speak with attitude to parents and siblings	Monitor during conversations throughout the day	10
	Daily total:	**0–18 tokens**

Positive Reinforcement With Praise

Praise is a wonderful way to positively impact your child's life and condition them to repeat praiseworthy behaviors. Giving praise seems simple, but the truth of the matter is that you can get it wrong.

For instance, overpraising your child by complimenting everything they do can be counterproductive. Your words, although encouraging, may start to lose their significance, and hearing them won't bring about effective change in your child's behavior. An example would be saying "Good job!" after every task your child completes. On the first few occasions, they may very well believe they have done a good job, but after a while, it starts to sound generic.

Another common mistake is praising your child's innate abilities, rather than their positive behavior. For example, if they perform well on a test, you might say "You are so smart!" On the surface, praising their abilities seems encouraging, but what happens when they perform poorly on the following test? They tell themselves that it's either they are smart or not smart, and base their sense of self-worth on their performance. This can lead to the fear of failure, perfectionism, or insecurities.

Praise should also focus on progress made, not results achieved. Noticing the small improvements your child makes is what encourages them to continue bettering themselves. It is about doing their best, not being the best that counts. Ultimately, children need to adopt a growth mindset, where they see their lives as a continuous process of learning. Praising their milestones, no matter how small they are, can help them develop resilience.

When done right, praise can boost your child's intrinsic motivation and set them on the path of personal mastery. Here are a few examples of the type of praise that positively impacts your child:

1. Sincere praise

We teach children that honesty is the best policy, but this standard applies for us too. Praise shouldn't paint a false picture of your child, or be inconsistent with how they see themselves. Instead, it should be based on behaviors you have seen and desire to highlight. When praise is too good to be true, your child can start to doubt their competence and become self-critical. Therefore, always seek to validate what your child can recognize in themselves too.

Example: "It was kind of you to help the other child off the swing."

2. Specific praise

Have you ever received a thoughtful gift from a friend or family member? How did it make you feel? I can imagine that what mattered most wasn't the size of the gift, but the fact that they had been listening all along. When your child receives generic praise like "That was awesome!" it can come across as insincere and as though you were not really paying attention to the actions they took. It would be the same as receiving a pair of socks or a tie for your birthday—good gifts, but what is the significance?

Whenever you decide to praise your child, get into the habit of describing what you saw them do which is praiseworthy. Be as specific as possible, so that they know what behaviors to repeat next time. Not only will this type of praise make them feel seen, they will also remember your words.

Example: "I like the color scheme you chose for your outfit. Good eye!"

3. Progress praise

Progress praise focuses on the efforts your child makes every day to learn a skill, develop a habit, or work toward a goal. Receiving praise like this can be incredibly motivating because your child has control over the amount of effort they invest. It can also foster a growth mindset that will help your child believe in their ability to overcome challenges, rather than focusing on their limitations.

Example: "I can see that you are working really hard on calming yourself when you feel upset."

4. Unconditional praise

Praise should never be tied to your expectations as a parent, or societal expectations that you desire for your child to uphold. It should focus on celebrating who your child is and accepting them as they are. Unconditional praise has no criteria before it is given. For instance, your child doesn't need to be a "good boy" or receive an A on their test before they are shown appreciation. Moreover, it doesn't seek to make your child become something they are not.

For instance, "I know you can do better than this" creates an expectation for your child to live up to your performance goals, not theirs. It also doesn't recognize the effort they have made to get to this point. A better compliment would be, "You did the best that you could and that makes me happy."

5. Spontaneous praise

Spontaneous praise can give your child a strong kick of dopamine. Since they are not expecting the encouraging words, hearing them can feel that much more rewarding. It also makes your praise sound genuine, since it is given randomly. The best way to give spontaneous praise is to pay attention to your child's behaviors. Get to know their positive and negative qualities, likes and dislikes, fears and ambitions, etc. Whenever you notice positive change, take the opportunity to say something.

You can also find creative ways of giving praise so that you aren't presenting it in the same form all of the time. For example, instead of giving your child a compliment, you can write a small note, bake their favorite cookies, or give them a big hug. What matters is being authentic however you choose to praise your child.

Example: "I like the way you handled that conflict with your friends. It showed a lot of maturity."

Chapter Takeaways

- The ADHD brain needs ongoing stimulation to maintain focus and dedication to tasks. This means that, unlike neurotypical children, your child craves a constant stream of motivation to carry out desirable behaviors.

- One of the ways to ensure that your child is frequently motivated is to create a rewards system at home. Rewards are an incredibly effective way to encourage desirable behaviors. They provide an incentive to work on building healthy habits.

- When creating a reward system, focus on target behaviors that need to be addressed urgently (behaviors that you would like your child to improve) then select the most suitable rewards, and the criteria for earning them (e.g., practicing desirable behavior three times a week to earn a reward).

- There are different types of reward systems that work best for young and older children. A behavioral chart is an easy-to-follow system that visually depicts good behaviors and the rewards for practicing them. A token economy works on a currency system, and allows your older child to earn and exchange tokens on a daily or weekly basis for equivalent rewards.

- A simple yet meaningful way to reward your child on a regular basis is to offer praise. Remember not to fall into the traps of overpraising, focusing on your child's abilities (rather than behavior), or praising positive outcomes (rather than progress). The best kind of praise is sincere, specific, unconditional, and spontaneous!

Chapter 10:

Exercises and Journal Prompts

There are two lasting bequests we can give our children. One is roots. The other is wings. –Hodding Carter, Jr.

Sensory-Seeking Indoor Activities

Sensory-seeking children enjoy exploring the world around them. Not only do they want to see with their eyes, they want to touch, taste, listen, and smell everything that their environment has to offer. Satisfying your child's need for stimulation can be easy outdoors, since there is so much nature and action available. However, when your child is indoors, they may frequently complain about being bored, or find unconstructive ways to spend their time. The following activities are great indoor solutions to keep your child active and engaged.

Play-Dough

Suitable age group: 3–8 years old

Instructions: Play-dough is a fun activity that allows your child's mind to run wild. Besides developing their fine motor skills, it can also enhance social skills. There are so many creative ways to manipulate play-dough. For example, you can challenge your child to create a pinch pot, make play-dough people or food, or make stamps and cut-outs using Lego and different toys.

While this activity appeals to children who enjoy touch, it can be unpleasant for those who are sensitive to scents (play-dough can have a strong smell) or those who like to put everything in their mouths. To prevent triggers, find easy-to-make play-dough recipes online (with edible ingredients).

Twister

Suitable age group: 9–12 years old

Instructions: Twister is a high-energy game that can also serve as a great workout for you and your child. The purpose of the game is to follow a set of instructions, telling each player where to move their hands and legs. The first player to fall on the ground is out. Since Twister requires following instructions, you may need to familiarize your child with the rules and do a practice run so that they know what to do.

Indoor Ball Pit

Suitable age group: 3–8 years old

Instructions: If you have open space inside your house, like an empty basement or room, you can create your own ball pit. Making one is incredibly simple: All you need is a blow-up kiddies pool and plastic balls from your local toy shop. Hide a few toys and pieces of candy inside the pit and ask your child to find as many as they can, blindfolded! The ball pit can also be used for pretend play. For instance, your child can imagine they are taking a few laps in the pool, taking a bath, or fishing in a lake.

Jell-O Painting

Suitable age group: 3–8 years old

Instructions: To make artwork that smells good and has an interesting texture, you can encourage your child to try Jell-O painting. There are a few ingredients that you will need before you start, such as: a few sachets of your child's favorite Jell-O, white glue, water, and a hard piece of cardboard.

Take out a plastic cup for each sachet of Jell-O. Pour 1 teaspoon of Jell-O, 1 tablespoon of water, and 1 tablespoon of white glue together. Mix each cup until you have a gooey texture. Drop a teaspoon of each mixture on random spots on the cardboard, then give your child a paintbrush (or let them use their fingers) to create different strokes and patterns.

Make as many mixtures as you need to complete the artwork then leave it outside to dry. Your child can reactivate the Jell-O smell by rubbing their fingers on the painting.

Sensory Box

Suitable age group: 3–8 years old

Instructions: Sensory-seeking children love to touch and experiment with their hands. If they cannot play in the garden with the dirt, you can create a sensory box that feels just as stimulating!

Identify their favorite texture to touch and manipulate. A few suggestions include sand, flour, beans, or rice. Purchase a plastic storage bin the size of a shoe box, and pour the ingredient about halfway. Add a few random toys and utensils your child can use to scoop, stack, and mix items together.

Self-Control Exercises and Prompts

Self-control helps your child regulate their emotions and choose the right behaviors during stressful situations. Instead of acting on their impulses, they are conditioned to stop, pause, and assess the right decisions to make. The best way to teach self-control is to help your child recognize that they are responsible for their actions. Below are a few exercises that can reinforce this idea.

Pros and Cons

Suitable age group: 9–17 years old

Instructions: Whenever your child is faced with a decision, ask them to grab a piece of paper and weigh the pros and cons of two choices. The pros are the benefits that come with a particular choice and the cons are the drawbacks.

Here is an example of how to weigh the pros and cons of two choices:

Decision: How do I confront a friend who is talking badly about me behind my back?			
Choice 1: Stop talking to them		Choice 2: Meet up to discuss my concerns	
Pros	Cons	Pros	Cons
I won't have to worry about being betrayed again.	They won't understand how hurt I feel.	I can confront them and express how I feel.	I am nervous to open up and share my feelings.
I can teach them a lesson not to talk badly about me again.	I run the risk of losing a good friend.	I can set boundaries and make the consequences of repeat behavior clear.	I am afraid my friend will be defensive and won't hear me out.

Reflecting On Decisions

Suitable age group: 13–17 years old

Instructions: At the end of each day, ask your child to grab their journal and reflect on the decisions they made, and how they can make better decisions tomorrow. Below are a few journal prompts they can answer:

1. Write down three decisions you made today.

_____

_____

_____

_____

2. Out of the three, which one is the *best decision* you made, and why?

_____

_____

_____

_____

3. How did the good decision positively impact your thoughts, feelings, or behaviors? For example, did it help you focus, make you feel confident, or improve your time management?

_____

_____

_____

_____

4. Out of the three, which one is the *worst decision* you made, and why?

_____

_____

_____

_____

5. How did the worst decision negatively impact your thoughts, feelings, or behaviors? For example, did it make you feel down, create conflict between you and others, or encourage bad habits?

_____

_____

_____

_____

6. Write down a few creative ideas to prevent repeating the worst decision tomorrow.

_____

_____

_____

_____

Think It or Say It?

Suitable age group: 9–17 years old

Instructions: Not everything that you think is appropriate to blurt out loud. Some thoughts are neither useful nor encouraging to you and others. It is important for your child to learn how to decide what to say and what to keep to themselves. Ask your child to take each sentence below and fit it under the most appropriate category: think it or say it. When they are done, look at how they were able to organize the sentences and whether they were placed under the correct categories. Take the opportunity to discuss real-life scenarios of when your child would find themselves in each situation.

1. Your outfit looks lovely today.

2. You talk funny.

3. I don't feel like speaking right now.

4. I don't like you.

5. I don't understand what you said.

6. I am confused.

7. I am smarter than you.

8. You smell.

9. Do you mind if I sit next to you?

10. Do you like me?

Think It	Say It

Identifying Self-Control Behaviors

Suitable age group: 9–17 years old

Instructions: Another way to help your child become aware of what self-control looks like is to assess their own behaviors. Ask your child to go through the list of behaviors below and assign them to the most appropriate category. When they have completed the exercise, check to see whether their sorting was correct. Take the opportunity to discuss why these behaviors are examples of self-control, or not.

1. You express to someone how angry you feel about their behavior and ask for an apology.

2. You yell at your mom for delaying cooking dinner.

3. You are having a bad day and decide to spend time alone in your room.

4. Someone made you upset so you look for ways to make them upset too.

5. You play video games before sitting down to do your homework.

6. You interrupt your friend while they are talking because you are bored.

7. You slam your bedroom door because you are angry.

8. You decide to save up money to purchase a gadget you really like.

9. You make it clear that you don't like somebody by ignoring them.

10. You decide not to do your chores because you don't
feel like it.

Self-Control	Lack of Self-Control

In Control/Out of Control

Suitable age group: 9–17 years old

Instructions: Not everything in life is within our control. There are certain situations that your child will experience which are out of their control, and some which are within their control. For example, they cannot control the weather, but they can control what outfit they choose to wear each day. Once they have decided what is within and outside of their control, they can learn to focus on those factors they can fix or change. Ask your child to go through the list of factors and decide which ones are within or outside of their control, or both. Thereafter, go through the table together and discuss.

1. Heart rate (fast or slow)

2. People's opinions

3. Submission deadline for tests

4. Throwing a tantrum

5. Being treated poorly by others

6. Choosing friends

7. Being focused on a task

8. Going to college after high school

9. Becoming a millionaire

10. Working hard at school

In Control	Out of Control	Both

Healthy Habits Exercises and Prompts

Healthy habits promote behaviors that can help your child manage their ADHD symptoms. However, before they can adopt healthy habits, they need to first identify and replace bad ones. The following exercises seek to help your child reflect on their habits and begin the process of breaking bad habits and adopting positive ones.

Reflecting On Current Habits

Suitable age group: 13–17 years old

Instructions: Think about the daily habits you practice and how they impact your life. Start by answering the following journal prompts, then create a list of helpful and harmful habits.

1. What behavior/activity do you spend the most time on each day? Does this activity improve your life in some way?

_____

_____

_____

_____

_____

_____

_____

2. What behaviors/activities would you say are time-wasters (they eat up your time and don't bring any positive growth)?

_____

_____

_____

_____

3. What behaviors/activities make you feel healthy each day?

_____

_____

_____

_____

4. Do you often procrastinate? If so, which tasks do you often procrastinate for?

_____

_____

_____

_____

_____

_____

5. What coping mechanisms help you calm down and feel positive each day?

_____

_____

_____

_____

6. Do you practice any bad coping mechanisms that put you in a bad mood, promote destructive behavior, or make you withdraw from people?

_____

_____

_____

_____

After completing the journal prompts, ask your child to fill out the following table by creating a list of helpful and harmful habits.

Helpful Habits	Harmful Habits

Helpful Habits	Harmful Habits

Breaking the Negative Habit Loop

Suitable age group: 13–17 years old

Instructions: In Chapter 5, we explored the three stages of habit formation: cue, routine, and reward. The beauty about understanding this process is that you can assist your child in breaking bad habits. Complete the following steps together:

1. Identify a bad habit that your child wants to break.

2. Write down the cue for the behavior (what triggers them to behave that way).

3. Write down the step-by-step routine carried out.

4. Write down the reward, or pleasurable feeling that is received after carrying out the routine.

5. Write down five ways to avoid the cue/trigger.

6. Write down five healthy behaviors that can bring the same desirable rewards.

Describe bad behavior in one sentence:	
What is the cue (trigger)?	
What is the step-by-step routine?	

What are the rewards?	
List five ways to avoid the trigger.	
List five healthy behaviors that can bring the same rewards.	

Copy this table and repeat the same process for other bad habits you may want to address.

Planning for Positive Habits

Suitable age group: 9–17 years old

Instructions: Adopting new habits requires a lot of commitment. Not only do you need to train your brain to behave differently, you need to keep yourself encouraged to do the right thing, even when you are tempted to fall back on bad behavior. The following questions will help your child create a plan for positive habits they would like to work on. When they are done, discuss their plan and ask for ways to support them.

1. Write down five positive behaviors you would like to turn into a habit.

_____

_____

_____

_____

2. Write down the benefits of making these behaviors new habits. For instance, how do you imagine they will change your life? What can you gain?

_____

_____

_____

_____

3. Write down negative consequences of not adopting these habits. For instance, if these behaviors don't become new habits, what would you lose? How would it negatively impact your life?

_____

_____

_____

_____

4. Write down daily action steps that can help you stay committed to these behaviors. Make sure the action steps are simple enough to practice every day.

_____

_____

_____

_____

5. Write down the cue, routine, and reward for each action step that will help your brain remember and desire to practice them regularly.

Here is an example:

New behavior: Waking up at 06:30 a.m. on weekdays

New action step: Going to bed at 09:30 every night

Cue: Alarm rings at 08:30 p.m.

Routine: Take a shower, brush my teeth, get into my pajamas, set out my clothes for tomorrow, then go to bed

Reward: Feeling rested and energized in the morning

_____

_____

_____

_____

6. List three people who can support you during the process of learning this new behavior/activity. Make sure you tell them about your plan and what you intend on doing each day to reinforce the behavior.

_____

_____

_____

_____

_____

_____

Healthy Habits Chart

Suitable age group: 9–17 years old

Instructions: Based on the action steps you came up with in the previous exercise, create a habit chart to keep you accountable for practicing those steps every day. Place a tick next to each action step you were able to accomplish by the end of the day.

Below is an example of how your habit chart should look:

	Mon	Tues	Wed	Thurs	Fri
Going to bed at 09:30 p.m.					

	Mon	Tues	Wed	Thurs	Fri
Sitting at my desk for 15 minutes					
Taking deep breaths when I am upset					
Writing about my day in my journal					
Allowing others to speak without interrupting them					

Communication Exercises and Prompts

Communication skills play a significant role in your child's development. Not only do they help him articulate his own thoughts and feelings, they can also help build and nurture relationships with others. The following exercises share some fun techniques that can improve your child's communication skills.

Telephone

Suitable age group: 3–8 years old

Instructions: Get the family together and sit in a circle. Make sure that you are close enough to each other to whisper in the next person's ear. One person begins the game by repeating a short sentence in their neighbor's ear. The message is passed on from one person to the next, until it reaches the last player. The last player shares the message out loud and the aim is to see how similar it sounds to the original message.

Picture Storytelling

Suitable age group: 3–8 years old

Instructions: Go through a magazine or picture book without text, and ask your child to create a story about what is happening in each photo. They can mention the location, action that is taking place, emotions of each character, and what they believe will occur next.

Mirroring

Suitable age group: 9–17 years old

Instructions: Sit facing your child and decide who is going to be the follower and the leader. The leader picks up a stack of flashcards with labels of different emotions. Without revealing the card, their challenge is to mime the emotion using their facial expressions (strictly no words). The follower is supposed to guess what emotion is being mimed. After a few rounds, the roles are switched and the leader becomes the follower, and vice versa. This game seeks to help your child recognize nonverbal communication.

Fists

Suitable age group: 9–17 years old

Instructions: Put one hand into a fist and challenge your child to get you to open the fist. However, the trick is not to use aggression (e.g., prying the fist open), but instead to use assertive communication. For example, "Open the fist!" won't bring successful outcomes, but "Please may you open the fist" might. Have fun encouraging your child to experiment with different assertive phrases.

DESO Script Scenarios

Suitable age group: 13–17 years old

Instructions: In chapter 7, we discussed an assertive communication technique known as the DESO script. This script can be used to express concerns, set boundaries, and resolve conflict with people. The following scenarios present real-life situations that your child may find themselves in. Encourage them to write down the best responses using the DESO script.

1. You are at a busy restaurant and the server is taking a long time to get to your table. How would you respond to them using the DESO script?

2. Your teacher returns a graded test that you feel should have earned a higher mark. How do you express your concern using the DESO script?

3. One of your friends teases you in front of a group of people. How can you express your hurt feelings using the DESO script?

4. Your parents have assigned you a chore that you dislike. How can you negotiate with them using the DESO script?

_____

_____

5. You are out in a public space and a stranger is standing too
   close to you. How can you set boundaries using the DESO
   script?

_____

_____

_____

_____

Conclusion

Sometimes parents are a channel to the larger society, sometimes they are a shield from it. Ideally, they act as filters, guiding their children and teaching them to avoid the tempting trash. –Dr. Louise Hart

Raising a hyperactive and impulsive boy is no easy feat. At times, you will feel overwhelmed by the constant need to monitor your child's behaviors at home and at school, the need to pay close attention to sensory triggers they may be exposed to, and having to gently respond to frequent emotional outbursts.

However, what is important to remember, especially during those moments when your energy is running low and you are close to having a meltdown too, is that ADHD symptoms do not define your child. Behind those symptoms is a human being who is struggling to express their needs. Perhaps if they knew to say "I am tired," or "I don't feel safe here," they would have better control over their emotions and urges.

You cannot change your child, nor can you take away their hyperactivity or impulsivity, but you can teach them how to self-regulate and take responsibility for their actions. At each stage of life, your child is able to learn new cognitive, emotional, and social skills. Your job as a parent is to introduce, teach, and reinforce those skills using age-appropriate strategies. Practicing once isn't enough to turn a desirable behavior into a habit. It takes countless practice—and positive reinforcement—to get your child to a point where they can practice the desirable behavior on their own.

The purpose of this guide is to help you see hyperactive-impulsive ADHD from a different perspective, and feel more confident in your ability to raise a healthy, happy, and responsible boy. The strategies presented in this book promote positive parenting principles that have been found effective in helping children with ADHD modify their behaviors.

The truth of the matter is that your child desires to be good, but requires extra support in learning what "good behavior" looks like, and how and when it should be practiced. You are the best mentor to prepare your child for adulthood and teach them everything they need to know about navigating through life.

If you have enjoyed the read, please leave an honest review! Your review will not only help me grow as an author but will also assist other individuals seeking guidance on their parenting journeys. Scan below to head on to the review page!
Thank you for your time and support.

About the Author

Richard Bass is a well-established author with extensive knowledge and background on children's disabilities. Richard has also experienced firsthand many children and teens who deal with depression and anxiety. He enjoys researching techniques and ideas to better serve students, as well as providing guidance to parents on how to understand and lead their children to success.

Richard wants to share his experience, research, and practices through his writing, as it has proven successful to many parents and students.

Richard feels there is a need for parents and others around the child to fully understand the disability, or the mental health of the child. He hopes that with his writing people will be more understanding of children going through these issues.

Richard Bass has been in education for over a decade and holds a bachelor's and master's degree in education as well as several certifications, including Special Education K-12 and Educational Administration.

Whenever Richard is not working, reading, or writing he likes to travel with his family to learn about different cultures as well as get ideas from all around about the upbringing of children, especially those with disabilities. Richard also researches and learns about different educational systems around the world.

Richard participates in several online groups where parents, educators, doctors, and psychologists share their success with children with disabilities. Richard is in the process of growing a Facebook group where further discussion about his books and techniques could take place. Apart from online groups, he has also attended training regarding the upbringing of students with disabilities and has also led training in this area.

A Message from the Author

If you enjoyed the book and are interested on further updates or just a place to share your thoughts with other readers or myself, please join my Facebook group by scanning below!

If you would be interested on receiving a FREE Planner for kids PDF version, by signing up you will also receive exclusive notifications to when new content is released and will be able to receive it at a promotional price. Scan below to sign up!

Scan below to check out my content on You Tube and learn more about Neurodiversity!

References

Ackerman, C. (2017, February 3). 25 Fun mindfulness activities for children and teens (+tips!). PositivePsychology.com. https://positivepsychology.com/mindfulness-for-children-kids-activities/

Aly. (2021, August 5). ADHD Behavior charts. Goally. https://getgoally.com/blog/adhd-behavior-charts/

Astray, T. (2020, March 19). Communication tool: Assertive confrontation and boundary setting with the DESO script. Tatiana Astray. http://www.tatianaastray.com/managing-relationships/2020/3/18/communication-tool-assertive-confrontation-and-boundary-setting-with-the-deso-script

AZ Quotes. (n.d.). Top 25 social skills quotes (of 51). A-Z Quotes. https://www.azquotes.com/quotes/topics/social-skills.html

Bailey, E. (2008, November 8). Using token economies to help manage behavior. Health Central. https://www.healthcentral.com/article/using-token-economies-to-help-manage-behavior

Borba, M. (2012, January 26). 7 Tricks to help stressed moms chill out. Today.com.

https://www.today.com/parents/7-tricks-help-stressed-moms-chill-out-1c7397996

Brain Balance. (n.d.). Sensory integration ideas for sensory seeking behaviors. Www.brainbalancecenters.com. https://www.brainbalancecenters.com/blog/sensory-integration-ideas-for-a-sensory-seeker

Branson, R. (2017, March 22). Everybody is a genius. Virgin.com. https://www.virgin.com/branson-family/richard-branson-blog/everybody-genius

Brown, T. E. (2022, June 20). Exaggerated emotions: How and why ADHD triggers intense feelings. ADDitude. https://www.additudemag.com/slideshows/adhd-emotions-understanding-intense-feelings/#:~:text=%E2%80%9CChallenges%20with%20processing%20emotions%20start

Clarity Clinic. (2020, April 11). Self soothing 101: Soothe your anxieties away. Clarity Clinic. https://www.claritychi.com/self-soothing-anxieties-away/

Coste, B. (n.d.). Parenting quotes on discipline: On loving unconditionally. Www.positive-Parenting-Ally.com. https://www.positive-parenting-ally.com/quotes-on-discipline.html

Cullins, A. (2022a, October 8). 7 Ways to help kids cope with big life changes. Big Life Journal. https://biglifejournal.com/blogs/blog/help-kids-cope-big-life-changes

Cullins, A. (2022b, October 22). Key strategies to teach children empathy (sorted by age). Big Life Journal. https://biglifejournal.com/blogs/blog/key-strategies-teach-children-empathy#:~:text=5-7%20Years

Danneman, I. (2021, September 16). How to calm a sensory seeking child: SPD breaks for sensitive kids. Www.additudemag.com. https://www.additudemag.com/sensory-break-ideas/

Davies, L. (n.d.). Assertiveness training for children. Www.kellybear.com. https://www.kellybear.com/TeacherArticles/TeacherTip74.html

Day, A. N. (2020, April 21). Guide: Teaching kids assertive vs aggressive communication. Raising an Extraordinary Person. https://hes-extraordinary.com/communication-assertive-vs-aggressive

Donvito, T. (2022, December 2). 8 Compliments you seriously need to stop giving to your kids. Reader's Digest. https://www.rd.com/list/compliments-that-are-hurtful/

Duhigg, C. (2011). How habits work. Charles Duhigg. https://charlesduhigg.com/how-habits-work/

Eccountability. (2017). Habit formation worksheet. In Eccountability. https://eccountability.io/wp-content/uploads/2017/05/Habit-Formation-Worksheet.pdf?x30826

Gill, T., & Hosker, T. (2021, February 10). How ADHD may be impacting your child's social skills and what you can do to help. Www.foothillsacademy.org. https://www.foothillsacademy.org/community/articles /adhd-social-skills#:~:text=When%20children%20with%20ADHD %20enter

Good Reads. (n.d.-a). A quote from Divergent Mind. Www.goodreads.com. https://www.goodreads.com/quotes/10380093-high-stimulation-is-both-exciting-and-confusing-for-people-with

Good Reads. (n.d.-b). Praising children quotes (1 quote). Www.goodreads.com. https://www.goodreads.com/quotes/tag/praising-children

Gordon, A. M., & Barnes, C. M. (2020, March 31). How working parents can prioritize sleep. Harvard Business Review. https://hbr.org/2020/03/how-working-parents-can-prioritize-sleep#:~:text=Good%20sleep%20may%20also%20be

Gracias, A. (2018, April 24). Positive self-talk: Ways to teach your children, benefits of self-talk. Www.parentcircle.com. https://www.parentcircle.com/how-to-teach-children-positive-self-talk/article

Green, R. (2022, August 6). ADHD Symptom spotlight: Overstimulation. Verywell Mind.

https://www.verywellmind.com/adhd-symptom-spotlight-overstimulation-5323859

Happy Publishing. (n.d.). 61 Self-control quotes that can change your life. Happy Publishing. https://www.happypublishing.com/blog/self-control-quotes/

Hill, L. (2019, July 9). Transforming habits: How to help a child focus in the classroom. Blog.revibetech.com. https://blog.revibetech.com/transforming-habits-how-to-help-a-child-focus-in-the-classroom

Hot Ground Gym. (2022, February 2). 8 Effective ways to channel your child's energy. Www.hotgroundgym.com. https://www.hotgroundgym.com/blog/8-effective-ways-to-channel-your-childs-energy

Jackson, C. (2022, May 15). How to use a reward system for a child with ADHD. Www.joonapp.io. https://www.joonapp.io/post/reward-system-for-adhd-child

Jellinek, M. S. (2010, May 1). Don't let ADHD crush children's self-esteem. Www.mdedge.com. https://www.mdedge.com/psychiatry/article/23971/pediatrics/dont-let-adhd-crush-childrens-self-esteem

Kessler, Z. (2022, January 27). Overstimulated by life? 20 Ways to give your ADHD senses a break. ADDitude. https://www.additudemag.com/overstimulation-sensory-overload-strategies-adhd/

Know what to expect! The 8 stages of social development in children. (2011, September 10). Child Development

Institute. https://childdevelopmentinfo.com/child-development/erickson/

Lack, E. (2022, November 18). What's your discipline style? Parenting. https://www.greatschools.org/gk/articles/what-is-your-discipline-style/

Lancia, G. (2021, July 1). 12 Self-control activities for kids (incl. worksheets). PositivePsychology.com. https://positivepsychology.com/self-control-for-kids/#techniques

Lehman, J. (n.d.). Teach your child responsibility — 7 Tips to get started. Empowering Parents. https://www.empoweringparents.com/article/teach-your-child-responsibility-7-tips-to-get-started/

Li, P. (2022, October 24). 6 Proven ways to encourage kids effectively (without side effects). Parenting for Brain. https://www.parentingforbrain.com/words-of-encouragement-for-kids/

Little Steps. (2020, October 19). In the womb. Little Steps. https://littlesteps.co.za/in-the-womb/#:~:text=A%20natural%20self%2Dsoothing%20behaviour

Littman, E. (2022, May 18). Brain stimulation and ADHD/ADD: Cravings and regulation. Www.additudemag.com. https://www.additudemag.com/brain-stimulation-and-adhd-cravings-dependency-and-regulation/#:~:text=Key%20aspects%20of%20the%20 reward

Low, K. (2022, April 19). Why kids with ADHD need structure (and how to provide it). Verywell Mind. https://www.verywellmind.com/why-is-structure-important-for-kids-with-adhd-20747#:~:text=Having%20a%20routine%20can%20benefit

Matteson, N. (2018, July 24). ADHD and transitions: Change is tough; how to deal with it. Www.healthyplace.com. https://www.healthyplace.com/blogs/livingwithadultadhd/2018/7/adhd-and-transitions-change-is-tough-how-to-deal-with-it

Mcleod, S. (2018). Erik Erikson's stages of psychosocial development. Simply Psychology. https://www.simplypsychology.org/Erik-Erikson.html

Merriam-Webster. (2019). Definition of energy. Merriam-Webster.com. https://www.merriam-webster.com/dictionary/energy

Miller, C. (2023, January 12). ADHD and behavior problems. Child Mind Institute. https://childmind.org/article/adhd-behavior-problems/#:~:text=Tantrums%20and%20defiance%20are%20not

Miller, K. (2019, May 21). 39 Communication games and activities for kids and students. PositivePsychology.com.

https://positivepsychology.com/communication-activities-adults-students/#kindergarten

Morin, A. (n.d.). 8 Sensory-friendly indoor games and activities. Www.understood.org. https://www.understood.org/en/articles/8-sensory-friendly-indoor-games-and-activities

Naik, A. (2022, January 6). How to teach your kids to delay gratification and why it matters. Go Henry. https://www.gohenry.com/us/blog/financial-education/how-to-teach-your-kids-to-delay-gratification-and-why-it-matters

Oxford Learner's Dictionaries. (2023). Discipline. Www.oxfordlearnersdictionaries.com. https://www.oxfordlearnersdictionaries.com/definition/english/discipline_1

Popova, M. (2017, September 25). The courage to be yourself: E.E. Cummings on art, life, and being unafraid to feel. The Marginalian. https://www.themarginalian.org/2017/09/25/e-e-cummings-advice/#:~:text=%E2%80%9CTo%20be%20nobody%2Dbut%2D

Roth, E., & Weiss, K. (2021, October 14). Types of ADHD: Inattentive, hyperactive-impulsive, and more. Healthline. https://www.healthline.com/health/adhd/three-types-adhd#causes

Schwartz, B. (2022, November 25). Self-soothing: What it is, benefits, and techniques to get started. Choosing Therapy. https://www.choosingtherapy.com/self-soothing/

Seymour, K. E., Macatee, R., & Chronis-Tuscano, A. (2016). Frustration tolerance in youth with ADHD. Journal of Attention Disorders, 23(11), 1229–1239. https://doi.org/10.1177/1087054716653216

Shanker, S., & Barker, T. (2017). Self-reg: How to help your child (and you) break the stress cycle and successfully engage with life. Penguin Books. https://www.amazon.com/Self-Reg-Child-Stress-Successfully-Engage/dp/0143110411

Sippl, A. (2020, June 26). Executive functioning and challenging behavior. Lifeskillsadvocate.com. https://lifeskillsadvocate.com/blog/executive-functioning-challenging-behavior/

Smith, D. (2021, July 19). 3 Keys to starting a routine and the steps to building one. This Wondrous Life. https://thiswondrouslife.com/twl/3-keys-to-starting-a-routine-and-the-steps-to-building-one

Spina Horan, K. (2021, December 30). Sneaky sensory triggers in ADHD that no one talks about. Www.psychologytoday.com. https://www.psychologytoday.com/za/blog/the-reality-gen-z/202112/sneaky-sensory-triggers-in-adhd-no-one-talks-about

Strong, R. (2022, September 11). Can ADHD affect your empathy? Healthline. https://www.healthline.com/health/adhd/adhd-and-empathy#signs-of-low-empathy

Stutman, M. (2016, November 11). Great empathy quotes for kids and students. InspireMyKids. https://inspiremykids.com/great-empathy-quotes-kids-students-children/#:~:text=%E2%80%9CEmpathy%20grows%20as%20we%20learn

Stutman, M. (2021, September 21). The power of habit! Great habit quotes for kids. InspireMyKids. https://inspiremykids.com/great-habit-quotes-for-kids/

Sword, R. (2021, September 6). How to encourage children to express feelings and emotions. High Speed Training. https://www.highspeedtraining.co.uk/hub/how-to-encourage-children-to-express-feelings/

Twitter. (2022, July 2). ADDitude quote on Twitter. Twitter. https://twitter.com/ADDitudeMag/status/1543263665008287744

Understood Team. (n.d.). Understanding sensory processing disorder. Www.understood.org. https://www.understood.org/en/articles/understanding-sensory-processing-issues

WebMD Editorial Contributors. (2021, June 14). Symptoms of ADHD. WebMD. https://www.webmd.com/add-

adhd/childhood-adhd/adhd-
symptoms#091e9c5e80008077-1-3

Zapata, K. (2021, October 29). Parental burnout: What it is and how to cope. Healthline. https://www.healthline.com/health/parenting/parental-burnout

Image References

Burton, K. (2021a). Black father with son covering mouth with hand on sofa [Online image]. In Pexels. https://www.pexels.com/photo/black-father-with-son-covering-mouth-with-hand-on-sofa-6624428/

Burton, K. (2021b). Desperate screaming young boy [Online image]. In Pexels. https://www.pexels.com/photo/desperate-screaming-young-boy-6624327/

Cameron, J. M. (2020). Photo of woman teaching his son while smiling [Online image]. In Pexels. https://www.pexels.com/photo/photo-of-woman-teaching-his-son-while-smiling-4145355/

Danilyuk, P. (2021). Man playing with boy on carpet [Online image]. In Pexels. https://www.pexels.com/photo/man-playing-with-boy-on-carpet-8763039/

Fischer, M. (2020). Kids sitting beside a bookshelves [Online image]. In Pexels.

https://www.pexels.com/photo/kids-sitting-beside-a-bookshelves-5211434/

Fring, G. (2021). Fireman giving the cat to an adorable boy [Online image]. In Pexels. https://www.pexels.com/photo/fireman-giving-the-cat-to-an-adorable-boy-7155808/

Grabowska, K. (2021). A boy writing on a book [Online image]. In Pexels. https://www.pexels.com/photo/a-boy-writing-on-a-book-6958518/

Holmes, K. (2020). Pensive African American kid with notepad [Online image]. In Pexels. https://www.pexels.com/photo/pensive-african-american-kid-with-notepad-5905894/

Kampus Production. (2021a). A mother talking to her child [Online image]. In Pexels. https://www.pexels.com/photo/a-mother-talking-to-her-child-7078729/

Kampus Production. (2021b). A boy and her mother drawing together [Online image]. In Pexels. https://www.pexels.com/photo/a-boy-and-her-mother-drawing-together-7417143/

Karpovich, V. (2020). A boy hugging his parents [Online image]. In Pexels. https://www.pexels.com/photo/a-boy-hugging-his-parents-4609093/

Krukau, Y. (2020a). Charming child sweeping concrete pavement with broomstick [Online image]. In Pexels. https://www.pexels.com/photo/charming-child-sweeping-concrete-pavement-with-broomstick-4458033/

Krukau, Y. (2020b). A woman sitting on a bed with her son [Online image]. In Pexels. https://www.pexels.com/photo/a-woman-sitting-on-a-bed-with-her-son-6210214/

Mas, A. (2020). Happy little boy standing near trunk [Online image]. In Pexels. https://www.pexels.com/photo/happy-little-boy-standing-near-trunk-5623720/

Monstera. (2021). Crop unrecognizable black father disciplining adorable attentive son at home [Online image]. In Pexels. https://www.pexels.com/photo/crop-unrecognizable-black-father-disciplining-adorable-attentive-son-at-home-7114233/

Nilov, M. (2021a). A man and young boy brushing teeth together [Online image]. In Pexels. https://www.pexels.com/photo/a-man-and-young-boy-brushing-teeth-together-8307422/

Nilov, M. (2021b). Photo of a boy with red hair holding a white blanket [Online image]. In Pexels. https://www.pexels.com/photo/photo-of-a-boy-with-red-hair-holding-a-white-blanket-8654431/

Pidvalnyi, O. (2022). A boy sleeping with his teddy bear [Online image]. In Pexels. https://www.pexels.com/photo/a-boy-sleeping-with-his-teddy-bear-12955638/

Rodnae Productions. (2021a). A young boy taking picture with his mother [Online image]. In Pexels. https://www.pexels.com/photo/a-young-boy-taking-picture-with-his-mother-6849308/

Rodnae Productions. (2021b). A cute little boy holding plush toys [Online image]. In Pexels. https://www.pexels.com/photo/a-cute-little-boy-holding-plush-toys-8363720/

Samkov, I. (2022). A boy in gray long sleeves playing toys on his hands [Online image]. In Pexels. https://www.pexels.com/photo/a-boy-in-gray-long-sleeves-playing-toys-on-his-hands-8504379/

Made in USA - North Chelmsford, MA
1373485_9781958350140
06.12.2023 1203